Ancient Order of
Melchizedek

By Ken Johnson, Th.D.

Copyright 2020, by Ken Johnson, Th.D.

Ancient Order of Melchizedek
by Ken Johnson, Th.D.

Printed in the United States of America

ISBN – 13: 9798667898436

Unless otherwise indicated, Bible quotations are taken from the King James Version.

Contents

Introduction 5
What is a Melchizedekian Priest? 7
Melchizedekian History 11
   The Pre-Flood World 12
   The Flood to Abraham 22
   Abraham to Levi 32
   The Order of Levi 40
   Jesus and John the Baptist 45
Melchizedekian Theology 59
   Melchizedek in the Bible 60
   Psalm 110 61
   The Book of Hebrews 65
   Hebrews 5 67
   Hebrews 6 72
   Hebrews 7 76
   Hebrews 8 84
   King – Priests 89
Melchizedekian Prophecy 99
   The Patriarchs 100
   The Messiah 103
   The Apostasy 109
   Messiah's Covenant / Priesthood 113
   The Date of the First Coming 119
Other Books by Ken Johnson, Th.D. 125
Bibliography 129

Introduction

Many people ask, "Who was Melchizedek mentioned in Genesis 14? And why did he bless Abraham?"

In this book we will discover that the original priests God created through Adam, were both kings and priests. When anointed with the Holy Spirit, they were also prophets. These king-priest-prophets were called Melchizedekian priests.

We will look at the history, theology, and prophecy of the Melchizedekian priests from many sources. These will include books of the Bible (Genesis and the Psalms), Jewish history books (the Ancient Book of Jasher and Josephus), Dead Sea Scroll Testaments (authored by Noah, Levi, Kohath, Amram, Aaron, and others), other Dead Sea Scrolls (Enoch, Jubilees, 4QMelchizedek, and others), and documents from Elijah's School of the Prophets. We will also look at what the early church fathers taught about the Melchizedekian priesthood.

We will learn how Jacob split up the Melchizedekian priesthood into three parts. The kings of Israel would come through his son Judah, the priests through his son Levi, and the birthright (prophetical line) would go to Joseph. This was to continue until the Messiah would come and reestablish the Melchizedekian priesthood. During the dispensation of Moses, God judged any king of Israel who

Ancient Order of Melchizedek

tried to reestablish the Melchizedekian priesthood by adding the priesthood to his office. This amounted to saying that he was the promised Messiah.

When John the Baptist (who was of the priestly line of Zadok) baptized Jesus (who was a direct descendant of King David) into the priesthood, and the Holy Spirit came upon Him, this reestablished the long-lost Melchizedekian priesthood.

We will break this study up into three parts: Melchizedekian history, Melchizedekian theology, and Melchizedekian prophecy.

In the first section, we will pull together all the information we can gather about the history and practice of the ten Melchizedekian priests who have walked the earth.

In the second part, we will concentrate on the theology. What does all of this mean to Christians and Jews and what does it have to do with our salvation? We will do in-depth studies of Hebrews 5-8, Psalm 110, and the Epistles of Peter, Paul, and John.

In the last section, we will concentrate on the prophecies about the reestablishment of the Melchizedekian priesthood and the Messiah from the Dead Sea Scrolls themselves.

What is a Melchizedekian Priest?

The Apostle Paul gives the definition of the word "Melchizedek" in the book of Hebrews.

"To whom also Abraham gave a tenth part of all; first being by interpretation King of Righteousness, and after that also King of Salem, which is, King of peace;" *Hebrews 7:2*

The Hebrew word "melek" means "king" and the Hebrew word "zedek" means "righteous." Melchizedek is properly translated as "King of Righteousness." The word Melchizedek can also be translated as "King of the Zadok priests."

The priests who lived in Qumran were direct descendants of the Jewish high priest Zadok. They were priests of righteousness. They were waiting for the Teacher of Righteousness to come. This righteous teacher, or Zadok teacher, was the Messiah.

First, we need to see that there was a real person named Levi. He was one of the twelve sons of Jacob and became the father of the tribe of Levi. Only his descendants can be Levitical priests. So, there is a priestly "Order of Levi." Levi's son was Kohath. Kohath's son was Amram. Amram had two sons, Moses and Aaron. Aaron became the first high priest of the nation of Israel after the Egyptian Exodus.

Ancient Order of Melchizedek

Only direct descendants of Aaron can be Aaronic priests. So, there is a priestly "Order of Aaron." There is also a priestly "Order of Melchizedek."

The apostle Paul stated that Jesus was ordained after the Order of Melchizedek, not the Order of Aaron or the Order of Levi. Jesus is a Melchizedekian priest, not an Aaronic priest or Levitical priest. Some have tried to teach that the Melchizedekian priest who appeared to Abraham was a Christophany, a pre-incarnate appearance of Jesus Christ. But they fail to see that Jesus *became* a priest after the *order* of Melchizedek.

> "...even Jesus, having become a high priest forever after the order of Melchizedek."
> *Hebrews 6:20 MKJV*

What modern Rabbis teach about Melchizedek comes from the Talmud, which is also called the "oral law." Jesus called this the "tradition of the elders." This teaching says there was no "Order of Melchizedek." Melchizedek was the name of a man who happened to be a priest of the Most High God.

On the contrary, the Dead Sea Scrolls teach there never was a man named Melchizedek. Melchizedek was an order of priests.

The Levitical and Aaronic priests were just priests. The apostle Paul teaches that any kind of priest is a human picked to intercede with God on behalf of other people. The

What is a Melchizedekian Priest?

Melchizedekian priests were a combination of priest, king, and prophet.

The Dead Sea Scrolls give us many details about the history and practice of the ten Melchizedekian priests ranging from Adam to the Messiah, Jesus Christ.

Ancient Order of Melchizedek

Melchizedekian History

The Pre-Flood World

According to ancient sources, Adam was the first king-priest-prophet. In this chapter we will trace the history of the Melchizedekian priests from Adam down to Noah. Here is their history.

Adam
Scripture says that God created Adam and gave him dominion over all the earth. This makes him king over the entire earth.

> "And God said, Let us make man in our image, after our likeness: and let them have dominion over the fish of the sea, and over the fowl of the air, and over the cattle, and over all the earth, and over every creeping thing that creepeth upon the earth. So God created man in His own image, in the image of God created He him; male and female created He them. And God blessed them, and God said unto them, Be fruitful, and multiply, and replenish the earth, and subdue it: and have dominion over the fish of the sea, and over the fowl of the air, and over every living thing that moveth upon the earth." *Genesis 1:26-28*

We know God talked with Adam and revealed to him that there was a need for a savior. God told him one of his descendants would be that savior.

The Pre-Flood World

"And I will put enmity between thee and the woman, and between thy seed and her seed; it shall bruise thy head, and thou shalt bruise His heel." *Genesis 3:15*

Jewish historian Josephus stated that God revealed to Adam there would be times of an apostasy followed by a destruction of the earth. Adam recorded this in his Testament. We do not have the Testament of Adam in its entirety from the Dead Sea Scrolls, but we have fragments of most of the testaments. Adam testified that destruction would happen once by a flood of water and once by fire, but apparently he was unsure which would occur first. Josephus records that Adam said:

> "the world was to be destroyed at one time by the force of fire, and at another time by the violence and quantity of water." Josephus' *Antiquities 1.2.3*

Adam was the king and a prophet, but was he also a priest? Genesis gives us a clue to answer this question. Moses records that both Cain and Abel knew a blood sacrifice was required, performed in a certain manner, at a predetermined place and time.

> "And in process of time it came to pass, that Cain brought of the fruit of the ground an offering unto the LORD. And Abel, he also brought of the firstlings of his flock and of the fat thereof. And the LORD had respect unto Abel and to his offering:" *Genesis 4:3,4*

Ancient Order of Melchizedek

The phrase "process of time" is thought to be an idiom. The Hebrew literally says, "after the end of the day." It is thought to indicate the year's end. The meaning is that at the appointed day (New Year's Day, Nisan 1), and place (the entrance to Eden), every male priest would return and give a blood sacrifice. The question this: here is where did Abel and Cain learn to give a proper blood offering and a proper grain offering? This would either be from God Himself or from Adam. In either case, we see the priesthood here in the text.

Seth

After Cain murdered Abel and fled, it was obvious that neither of them would be the next Melchizedekian priest-king. When Adam was one hundred and thirty years old, he had a son whom he named Seth. This would be the Jewish year 130 AM. Seth was righteous, but there was no indication that Seth was to be the promised Messiah or the next King of Righteousness.

Enos

When Seth was one hundred and five years old, he had a son whom he named Enos. This would have been 235 AM. Enos was godly, but it is recorded that in his days there was an apostasy.

> "And it was in the days of Enosh [Enos] that the sons of men continued to rebel and transgress against God, to increase the anger of the Lord against the sons of men. And the sons of men went and they served other gods, and they forgot the Lord who had

created them in the earth: and in those days the sons of men made images of brass and iron, wood and stone, and they bowed down and served them. And every man made his god and they bowed down to them, and the sons of men forsook the Lord all the days of Enosh and his children; and the anger of the Lord was kindled on account of their works and abominations which they did in the earth." *Ancient Book of Jasher 2:3-5*

Cainan

When Enos was ninety years old, he had a son whom he named Cainan. This would have been 325 AM. When Cainan was forty years old, in 365 AM, he became wise in the things of God and prophecy. He understood that the water destruction would come first. He was just not sure when it would happen. Notice that Cainan wrote these things down in his testament.

> "And Cainan grew up and he was forty years old, and he became wise and had knowledge and skill in all wisdom, and he reigned over all the sons of men, and he led the sons of men to wisdom and knowledge… And Cainan knew by his wisdom that God would destroy the sons of men for having sinned upon earth, and that the Lord would in the latter days bring upon them the waters of the flood. And in those days Cainan wrote upon tablets of stone, what was to take place in time to come, and he put them in his treasures." *Ancient Book of Jasher 2:11-13*

Ancient Order of Melchizedek

God sent minor floods and pestilences to get the people's attention; and then God used Cainan to start a revival. Seeing God's hand on Cainan, Adam made him the second king of the earth, the second King of Righteousness.

> "Cainan reigned over the whole earth, and he turned some of the sons of men to the service of God."
> *Ancient Book of Jasher 2:14*

The revival seems to be short lived. Cainan had a son whom he named Mahalaleel. Mahalaleel was born in 395 AM. Jasher says,

> "For in those days the sons of men began to trespass against God, and to transgress the commandments which he had commanded to Adam…"
> *Ancient Book of Jasher 2:19*

Enoch
While things were getting worse and worse with most of the people on earth, Mahalaleel had a son whom he named Jared and Jared had a son whom he named Enoch. Enoch was born in 622 AM. When Enoch grew up, he wholly followed the ways of the Lord and led another revival. Enoch's revival was much more successful than that of Cainan. Seeing God's hand move so mightily through Enoch, he was made the third King of Righteousness in 687 AM.

> "Enoch reigned over the sons of men two hundred and forty-three years, and he did justice and

righteousness with all his people, and he led them in the ways of the Lord." *Ancient Book of Jasher 3:12*

Notice how a true man of God will gladly step down if it fulfills prophecy. We should all be glad to be a part of God's plan, but be mindful to never be in a position of standing in His way.

God gave Enoch a prophecy that the Messiah would come seventy generations from his time. See *Ancient Book of Enoch 10*. Luke 3:23-38 verifies that Jesus Christ is the seventieth generation from Enoch.

Most followed Enoch, but not completely. Slowly he began to withdraw from political life and spend more and more time alone with God. In 987 AM, God raptured Enoch as the Scripture says:

"And Enoch walked with God: and he was not; for God took him." *Genesis 5:24*

Enoch was an amazing prophet. He named his son Methuselah. That name is made up of two Hebrew words: "meth" meaning "death" and "selah" meaning "to send." These two words put together form a Hebrew sentence. Methuselah's name means "when he is dead, it shall be sent." If you look carefully at the genealogical records given in Genesis 5, Jasher 5-6, and the Seder Olam 1, it is clear that Methuselah died in the year of the flood.

Ancient Order of Melchizedek

Methuselah

After Enoch's rapture, his son Methuselah was made the next King of Righteousness.

> "All the days that Enoch lived upon earth, were three hundred and sixty-five years. And when Enoch had ascended into heaven, all the kings of the earth rose and took Methuselah his son and anointed him, and they caused him to reign over them in the place of his father. And Methuselah acted uprightly in the sight of God, as his father Enoch had taught him, and he likewise during the whole of his life taught the sons of men wisdom, knowledge and the fear of God, and he did not turn from the good way either to the right or to the left." *Ancient Book of Jasher 4:1-3*

But it was not long until another apostasy came, and the people turned away from God and His ways.

> "But in the latter days of Methuselah, the sons of men turned from the Lord, they corrupted the earth, they robbed and plundered each other, and they rebelled against God and they transgressed, and they corrupted their ways, and would not hearken to the voice of Methuselah, but rebelled against him." *Ancient Book of Jasher 4:4*

Methuselah had a son whom he called Lamech. Lamech then had a son whom he named Noah. Noah was born in 1056 AM. We are not told much of Lamech, but Jewish legends state he was not very godly. Methuselah knew by

The Pre-Flood World

inspiration of the Holy Spirit that his grandson, Noah, would be the one. Not the Messiah who would be seventy generations from his father Enoch, but that Noah would be the next King of Righteousness.

Noah

Noah grew up and followed the ways of God as taught by his grandfather Methuselah. Noah was given all the patriarchal writings from Adam to his time. During this time even the descendants of Seth became corrupt.

"Now this posterity of Seth continued to esteem God as the Lord of the universe, and to have an entire regard to virtue, for seven generations; but in process of time they were perverted, and forsook the practices of their forefathers; and did neither pay those honors to God which were appointed them, nor had they any concern to do justice towards men. But for what degree of zeal they had formerly shown for virtue, they now showed by their actions a double degree of wickedness, whereby they made God to be their enemy." Josephus' *Antiquities 1.3.1*

In 1536 AM, God gave Noah a prophecy that man had one hundred and twenty years to repent or the flood judgment would occur. Methuselah and Noah preached repentance for the entire one-hundred-and-twenty-year period.

As a side note, you know neither one of these two godly men were stupid. After only a few years I think they realized there would be no revival this time. But they did

Ancient Order of Melchizedek

not stop because it was useless. Instead they continued, at least, to be an example of righteousness and a witness for future generations. If you are a minister and see no fruit yet, realize it is not your job to save people. It is your job to be a witness for Him. Do not stop doing what God has called you to do because you do not understand what is going on. Just be a witness.

Noah records in his Testament that he was told he would be the next King of Righteousness after the flood.

> "You will govern the entire earth; all that is upon it, including the mountains and the seas..."
> *Testament of Noah, Col. 7*

In column 10 of the Testament of Noah, Noah describes the offering he did as a priest. The atonement offering was a goat. The thank offering was an ox, ram, sheep, and turtledoves with salt. The meal offering was with wheat, oil and incense. This incense was most likely frankincense. So again, we see king, priest, and prophet in one person. This is a Melchizedekian priest.

> "I atoned for the whole earth. First, I offered a male goat... afterward I burned the fat upon the fire. Second, I offered a thank offering consisting of ox, ram, and sheep. Then I poured out all of their blood on the base of the altar, and burned all of their flesh on the altar. Third, I offered the young turtledoves (flesh and blood) with them upon the altar. Then I offered fine wheat flour, mixed together with oil

containing incense, for their meal offerings. I said a blessing, and was putting salt on all of them, and the scent of my offering rose up to the heavens."
Testament of Noah, Col. 10

The Flood occurred in 1656 AM. The fragments of the Testament of Noah that were found in the Dead Sea Scrolls reveal some interesting details for our study.

In column 8 it is written that Noah had the "written accounts" of the patriarchs with him aboard the ark.

At this point we have the preflood list of Melchizedekian priests, or king-priest-prophets. These include:

1. Adam,
2. Cainan,
3. Enoch,
4. Methuselah, and
5. Noah.

Conclusion
At the time of the Flood we have Noah, the fifth King of Righteousness (priest, king, and prophet) taking with him aboard the Ark all the patriarchal testaments. He knew the Messiah would come seventy generations after Enoch, which would be sixty-six generations after one of his three children. Which one of his children would the Messiah come from? He did not know. But he knew that through one of them a descendant would come to create a great nation that would usher in the reign of the Messiah.

Ancient Order of Melchizedek

The Flood to Abraham

After spending an entire year in the Ark, Noah and his family went out from the Ark in Nisan of the Jewish year 1657 AM.

> "And it came to pass in the six hundredth and first year, in the first month, the first day of the month, the waters were dried up from off the earth: and Noah removed the covering of the ark, and looked, and, behold, the face of the ground was dry."
> *Genesis 8:13*

After they left the Ark, Noah did sacrifice to God as we detailed in the last chapter.

> "And on the new moon of the third month he went forth from the ark, and built an altar on that mountain [Lubar]. And he made atonement for the earth, and took a kid and made atonement by its blood for all the guilt of the earth;" *Ancient Book of Jubilees 6:1,2*

> "And Noah builded an altar unto the LORD; and took of every clean beast, and of every clean fowl, and offered burnt offerings on the altar." *Genesis 8:20*

After Noah's sacrifice, God made a covenant with him and his sons. This is recorded in Genesis 9. It is referred to as the Rainbow Covenant, but it is properly called the

The Flood to Abraham

Noahide Covenant. God promised not to destroy the earth again with water and set the rainbow in the sky as a sign of the covenant between God and all of the Gentile nations (His creatures). God then instructed Noah to teach his sons to observe what became known as the Seven Noahide Laws.

They were commanded to spread out over the earth and create nations. Each Gentile nation was to create courts of justice, and to punish murder, theft, fornication, idolatry, and blasphemy. They were to add other laws as they saw fit for their individual countries, but never abolish the seven fundamental laws. Blasphemy was defined as not believing everything the prophets said about sin, salvation, and the coming Messiah. Most Gentile nations quickly became idolatrous and forgot the teachings of the prophets.

The *Testament of Noah* reveals that Noah had a prophetic dream about the end of his age. There would be an apostasy, an Antichrist figure, and one who would begin the holy nation who would usher in the prophesied Messiah.

Columns 13 through 15 of the *Testament of Noah* contain the dream. It is heavily fragmented, but we will recreate the clear parts here.

Noah saw a small cedar tree that grew into a large tree and filled the earth. He was told in the dream that he, as king of the earth, was that tree. Other Dead Sea Scrolls teach that cedar trees represent Gentile nations. This mighty tree had

Ancient Order of Melchizedek

three large branches that blossomed out. These represented Noah's three sons: Shem, Ham, and Japheth. The third branch had two small shoots that broke off and left the large branch. They went up to one of the other branches and started attacking it. They almost destroyed the upper branch, but a small twig from the upper branch separated itself and became an olive vine. The olive vine always represents the nation of believing Israel. This olive vine destroyed the attacking branches.

> "with one branch separating from it and becoming an olive tree means the first son will not separate from you for all his days, and among his seed your name will be called." *Ancient Testament of Noah, Col. 14*

Shem was to be the next King of Righteousness and guard against the coming invasion and apostasy. Shem would not be able to stop it, just slow it down and save those whom he could. Before the apostasy would be complete, one would arise from his seed and destroy the apostate kingdom.

There are other parts to the dream, but this will suffice for our study. The obvious interpretation is that the two evil twigs were Nimrod and Canaan. They invaded Shem's portion and came together to form a one-world empire and a one-world religion. Then God used Abraham to form the nation of Israel and through them the Messiah would eventually come.

The Flood to Abraham

> "Then I, Noah, awoke. It was morning and I blessed the everlasting God. I quickly went to Shem, my son, and told him everything, that through him the Righteous One would come, and that he had to preserve the knowledge and become the next priest of the Most High God."
>
> *Ancient Testament of Noah, Col. 15*

Noah ordained Shem to be the sixth Melchizedekian priest of the Most High God. Shem's son was Arphaxad, his grandson was Salah, and his great-grandson was Eber. Eber was born in 1723 AM, sixty-seven years after the Flood. His heart was perfect before the Lord his God. Was he to be the next King of Righteousness? Shem should wait until he could be sure. If God told Shem directly to anoint Eber as the next King of Righteousness he would, or if he witnessed Eber fulfilling the prophecy by destroying the apostasy, then he could be sure. But the growing apostasy was not yet full.

Shem and Eber kept the ancient records of their fathers that Noah had brought aboard the Ark and they wrote the historical records of their time. In time Eber was given a vision that a series of earthquakes would occur to further separate the nations. When Eber had his son, he named him Peleg which means "earthquake" in Hebrew.

Peleg's son was Reu, his grandson was Serug, his great-grandson was Nahor, and his great-great-grandson was Terah. Terah was born in 1878 AM. By now it was looking like the apostasy would not be fully developed and destroyed by a descendant of Shem until the end of the age (the year 2000 AM). But Shem had to live long enough to ordain the next King of Righteousness. Nimrod was born in 1908 AM. Nimrod was the son of Cush, and the grandson of Ham. By 1920 AM, Canaan already had a stronghold in Shem's land and Nimrod started attacking some of the Japhethites who lived at the most eastern parts of Shem's kingdom. By 1940 AM he had seized the throne of what would later be called Babylon, and welcomed the Canaanites under his rule.

> "Now it was Nimrod who excited them to such an affront and contempt of God. He was the grandson of Ham, the son of Noah, a bold man, and of great strength of hand. He persuaded them not to ascribe it to God, as if it was through his means they were happy, but to believe that it was their own courage which procured that happiness. He also gradually changed the government into tyranny, seeing no other way of turning men from the fear of God, but to bring them into a constant dependence on his power. He also said he would be revenged on God, if he should have a mind to drown the world again; for that he would build a tower too high for the waters to be able to reach! and that he would avenge himself on God for destroying their forefathers!"
> *Josephus' Antiquities 1.4.2*

Nimrod not only changed the government into a tyranny but instituted a pagan religious system involving ancestor

The Flood to Abraham

worship and religious rites connected with certain star patterns in the Zodiac.

Nimrod became an undisputed ruler and he made Terah a general in his army. When Terah was seventy years old, in 1948 AM, he had a son whom he called Abram. A prophecy was given at Abram's birth that he and his descendants would destroy Nimrod's kingdom.

Nimrod ordered the boy's death, but Terah secretly hid Abram until he was able to send him to the house of Noah which was still outside of Nimrod's reach.

> "And Abram was in Noah's house thirty-nine years, and Abram knew the Lord from three years old, and he went in the ways of the Lord until the day of his death, as Noah and his son Shem had taught him; and all the sons of the earth in those days greatly transgressed against the Lord, and they rebelled against him and they served other gods, and they forgot the Lord who had created them in the earth; and the inhabitants of the earth made unto themselves, at that time, every man his god; gods of wood and stone which could neither speak, hear, nor deliver, and the sons of men served them and they became their gods." *Ancient Book of Jasher 9:6*

When Abram was forty-nine years old, he went back to the house of his father. Abram convinced Terah to leave the idols and follow the Most Hight God. This angered Nimrod who sought to kill Abram. Abram and his family, along

Ancient Order of Melchizedek

with Terah and many people, fled from Nimrod and went to dwell in the city of Haran.

Nimrod would have pursued him to kill the entire group, but in 1997 AM, the providence of Elam led by Chedorlaomer rebelled against Nimrod. With Nimrod's full attention to this war, Abram and his people were left alone. At the end of the first age, 2000 AM, Nimrod had this dream.

"...the king fell asleep and dreamed that he was standing with his troops and hosts in a valley opposite the king's furnace. And he lifted up his eyes and saw a man in the likeness of Abram coming forth from the furnace, and that he came and stood before the king with his drawn sword, and then sprang to the king with his sword. When the king fled from the man, for he was afraid and while he was running, the man threw an egg upon the king's head, and the egg became a great river. And the king dreamed that all his troops sank in that river and died. And the king took flight with three men who were before him and he escaped. And the king looked at these men and they were clothed in princely dresses as the garments of kings, and had the appearance and majesty of kings. And while they were running, the river again turned to an egg before the king, and there came forth from the egg a young bird which came before the king, and flew at his head and plucked out the king's eye. And the king was grieved at the sight, and he

The Flood to Abraham

awoke out of his sleep and his spirit was agitated; and he felt a great terror."
Ancient Book of Jasher 12:45-50

The interpretation was given that Abram would cause the downfall of Nimrod's kingdom and a descendant of Abraham would kill Nimrod. This was God's last act toward Nimrod to cause him to repent.

The end of the age had come and gone and Shem did see Abram leading a small revival within his family and he did see the breakup of the empire but God had not directly spoken to Abram or Shem about the prophecy. Nimrod's empire was still partly present. So, Shem waited to see what God would do.

Eventually God did speak to Abram. God changed his name to Abraham and made the covenant with him. He was to be the next King of Righteousness and father the nation through whom the Messiah would come.

"Now the LORD had said unto Abram, Get thee out of thy country, and from thy kindred, and from thy father's house, unto a land that I will shew thee: And I will make of thee a great nation, and I will bless thee, and make thy name great; and thou shalt be a blessing: And I will bless them that bless thee, and curse him that curseth thee: and in thee shall all families of the earth be blessed." *Genesis 12:1-3*

Ancient Order of Melchizedek

Abraham was the fourteenth generation from Enoch; so the Messiah's coming was still quite a long way off.

As Chedorlaomer captured more territory, he took control of Sodom and Gomorrah and the cities of the plains. He slew all of the giant clans. He left a wake of complete destruction everywhere he went. In time, Sodom and the other cities of the plains rebelled against Elam. Chedorlaomer squelched the rebellion by slaughtering many and taking prisoners, among whom was Lot, Abraham's nephew. This was it! Surely the fulfillment of the prophecy was just around the corner. With Nimrod's kingdom diminished and Chedorlaomer on a rampage, could Abraham defeat Chedorlaomer and take control as prophesied? Abraham rose up, killed Chedorlaomer, slaughtered his forces, rescued his nephew Lot, and returned the captives to the cities.

Shem wasted no time coming down to Abraham to anoint him as the next Melchizedekian priest. Moses said this about the event.

> "And the king of Sodom went out to meet him after his return from the slaughter of Chedorlaomer, and of the kings that were with him, at the valley of Shaveh, which is the king's dale. And Melchizedek king of Salem brought forth bread and wine: and he was the priest of the most high God. And he blessed him, and said, Blessed be Abram of the most high God, possessor of heaven and earth: And blessed be the most high God, which hath delivered thine

The Flood to Abraham

enemies into thy hand. And he gave him tithes of all."
Genesis 14:17-20

Jasher says this about the event.

"And Bera king of Sodom, and the rest of his men that were with him, went out from the lime pits into which they had fallen, to meet Abram and his men. And Adonizedek king of Jerusalem, the same was Shem, went out with his men to meet Abram and his people, with bread and wine, and they remained together in the valley of Melech. And Adonizedek blessed Abram, and Abram gave him a tenth from all that he had brought from the spoil of his enemies, for Adonizedek was a priest before God."
Ancient Book of Jasher 16:10-12

The date given for this event was 2021 AM, which would make Abraham seventy-three years old.

Shem passed away at the age of six hundred, in 2158 AM. Eber then took full control of the School of the Prophets and continued their work teaching the whole council of God and recording history.

Conclusion
This makes Shem the sixth, and Abraham the seventh, Melchizedekian priest.

Abraham to Levi

Abraham was one hundred years old when he had a son whom he named Isaac. Moses taught that God swore in an oath that He would enter the next covenant with Isaac.

"And there was a famine in the land, beside the first famine that was in the days of Abraham. And Isaac went unto Abimelech king of the Philistines unto Gerar. And the LORD appeared unto him, and said, Go not down into Egypt; dwell in the land which I shall tell thee of: Sojourn in this land, and I will be with thee, and will bless thee; for unto thee, and unto thy seed, I will give all these countries, and I will perform the oath which I sware unto Abraham thy father; And I will make thy seed to multiply as the stars of heaven, and will give unto thy seed all these countries; and in thy seed shall all the nations of the earth be blessed; Because that Abraham obeyed my voice, and kept my charge, my commandments, my statutes, and my laws." *Genesis 26:1-5*

After the death of Sarah; Abraham buried her at the interment of kings. Many kings of the land attended her funeral, including Shem, Noah's son. Shem's sons Eber and Abimelech, together with Anar, Ashcol and Mamre were also there. Abraham recognized Isaac was ordained by God, so he sent him to learn the ways of God and how to be a priest of the Most High God.

Abraham to Levi

> "And when the days of their mourning passed by Abraham sent away his son Isaac, and he went to the house of Shem and Eber, to learn the ways of the Lord and his instructions, and Abraham remained there three years." *Ancient Book of Jasher 24:17*

Isaac always thought that Esau, his firstborn, would be the next priest, even though Isaac's father, Abraham, knew God had selected Jacob over Esau. This was actually easy for all to see. Jacob was a "man of the tents," meaning he loved to study the prophecies. It was well known that Esau could not care less for the things of God. But Isaac's mind was made up. Jacob should not have deceived his father Isaac. God would have made Jacob the next heir to the blessing no matter what.

> "And his father Isaac said unto him, Come near now, and kiss me, my son. And he came near, and kissed him: and he smelled the smell of his raiment, and blessed him, and said, See, the smell of my son is as the smell of a field which the LORD hath blessed: Therefore God give thee of the dew of heaven, and the fatness of the earth, and plenty of corn and wine: Let people serve thee, and nations bow down to thee: be lord over thy brethren, and let thy mother's sons bow down to thee: cursed be every one that curseth thee, and blessed be he that blesseth thee. And it came to pass, as soon as Isaac had made an end of blessing Jacob, and Jacob was yet scarce gone out from the presence of Isaac his father, that Esau his brother came in from his hunting." *Genesis 27:26-30*

Ancient Order of Melchizedek

What is interesting about the details of Genesis 27 is that even though Isaac's mind was set, he recognized God's hand on Jacob. As Americans we would say "he deceived me" and, therefore, my oath is null and void. But Jacob knew that if God wanted Esau to have the inheritance, God would have made it happen. God is in control. We should all learn that lesson from Jacob.

> "And it was after the death of Abraham that God blessed his son Isaac and his children, and the Lord was with Isaac as he had been with his father Abraham, for Isaac kept all the commandments of the Lord as Abraham his father had commanded him; he did not turn to the right or to the left from the right path which his father had commanded him."
> *Ancient Book of Jasher 26:39*

Esau would not repent and become a godly man. God had made it clear that His hand was on Jacob, so Isaac sent Jacob to study for the priesthood.

> "At that time Isaac sent his younger son Jacob to the house of Shem and Eber, and he learned the instructions of the Lord, and Jacob remained in the house of Shem and Eber for thirty-two years, and Esau his brother did not go, for he was not willing to go, and he remained in his father's house in the land of Canaan." *Ancient Book of Jasher 28:18*

Abraham to Levi

God spoke to Jacob and renewed the covenant with him as He did with Isaac his father. This happened in a dream Jacob had while in Bethel.

"And he dreamed, and behold a ladder set up on the earth, and the top of it reached to heaven: and behold the angels of God ascending and descending on it. And, behold, the LORD stood above it, and said, I am the LORD God of Abraham thy father, and the God of Isaac: the land whereon thou liest, to thee will I give it, and to thy seed; And thy seed shall be as the dust of the earth, and thou shalt spread abroad to the west, and to the east, and to the north, and to the south: and in thee and in thy seed shall all the families of the earth be blessed. And, behold, I am with thee, and will keep thee in all places whither thou goest, and will bring thee again into this land; for I will not leave thee, until I have done that which I have spoken to thee of. And Jacob awaked out of his sleep, and he said, Surely the LORD is in this place; and I knew it not." *Genesis 28:12-16*

Jacob studied with Shem and Eber at the School of the Prophets until the death of Shem in 2158 AM. Eber continued the school, but copies of all of the records were given to Levi for safe keeping. Eber died in 2187 AM, just twenty-nine years after his father, Shem, died. Shortly thereafter the area was overrun by the Amorites. They seized control of the area, took the records as their own, and even took the title of Adonaizedek (the Lord of Righteousness) as their own. They took the records seriously because by the time Joshua was making the conquest of the land of Canaan, the Amorites had reproduced clans of giants.

> "And it came to pass in those days, in the hundred and tenth year of the life of Isaac, that is in the fiftieth year of the life of Jacob, in that year died Shem the son of Noah; Shem was six hundred years old at his death. And when Shem died Jacob returned to his father to Hebron which is in the land of Canaan."
> *Ancient Book of Jasher 28:24-25*

In time Jacob had twelve sons. The eldest was Reuben, who should have inherited the promise, but he discredited himself through fornication. Jacob knew better than to do anything out of presumption, so he waited for the Lord to reveal to him what was to be done. At this time Levi, another son of Jacob, started having prophetic dreams and realized he needed to be saved!

> "I, Levi, was born in Haran. When I was young, my father moved us to Shechem. When I was about twenty, Simeon and I took vengeance on Hamor for our sister Dinah. One day we were feeding our flocks in Abel-Maul, and the spirit of understanding of the Lord came upon me, and I understood that all men corrupt their way, and that righteousness had retreated behind walls and iniquity ruled. I grieved for mankind, and I prayed to the Lord that I might be saved." *Testament of Levi 2*

Abraham to Levi

This is a very important point. Every human being is born with a sin nature and corrupts his or her ways. Every single person needs to be saved by believing in the revealed words of God through the prophets, and repenting of their sins. Once Levi understood this, he repented of his sins and God spoke to him in another dream.

> "The Most High has heard your prayer. Your sins are forgiven, and you will become a son to Him, a servant and minister of His presence. You will shine the light of knowledge to Jacob, a sun to the seed of Israel. You and all your seed will be blessed until the Lord visits all the heathen in the tender mercies of His Son, even forever." *Testament of Levi 4*

Notice also that those saved did not reveal everything they knew about God to unbelievers. They waited until God started a relationship with the unbelievers and revealed things to them. Only when this happens do we truly know what God is doing, and that makes it unlikely that we will be conned by any unbeliever. When Levi told Jacob about the dreams, Jacob knew Levi was chosen. God then revealed to Jacob what was to be done.

> "After two days Judah and I went up to Isaac after our father; and my grandfather blessed me according to all the words of the visions which I had seen. He would not come with us to Bethel. When we came to Bethel, my father Jacob had a vision concerning me, that I should become a priest unto the Lord; and he rose up early in the morning, and paid tithes of all to

the Lord through me. We came to Hebron to dwell there, and Isaac continually taught me the law of the Lord, even as the angel of God showed to me. He taught me the law of the priesthood, of sacrifices, whole burnt offerings, first-fruits, free will offerings, and thank offerings. Every day he instructed me, and prayed for me before the Lord." *Testament of Levi 9*

Jacob sent Levi to learn the priesthood from Isaac his father. God had revealed to Jacob that the Melchizedekian priesthood was to be broken up until the coming of the Messiah.

"At that time the portion of birthright, together with the kingly and priestly offices, was removed from the sons of Reuben, for he had profaned his father's bed, and the birthright was given unto Joseph, the kingly office to Judah, and the priesthood unto Levi, because Reuben had defiled his father's bed." *Ancient Book of Jasher 36:15*

The prophecies stated that the Messiah would be born a direct descendant of Judah. He would be born as King. Afterwards, Messiah would have to be ordained into the priesthood by a priest of that order. This was the only way for Him to become a real priest. He would also have to be filled with the Holy Spirit to become a prophet. Only with these three offices uniting into one man could the Melchizedekian priesthood be recreated.

Abraham to Levi

In the books of Kings and Chronicles, we read about some kings of Israel and Judah who tried to usurp the office of priest and were cursed of God for doing so. In effect, they were trying to make people believe they were the Messiah by restoring the ancient priesthood. But with Jesus, instead of being cursed, He was blessed with the Holy Spirit descending on Him in the form of a dove, proving God's blessing was on Him and testifying that He truly was the Messiah.

Ancient Order of Melchizedek

The Order of Levi

The priesthood part of the Order of Melchizedek was virtually the same as that of the newly created Order of Levi. Abraham had added the practice of circumcision to their laws. Jacob added some other stipulations. Moses would later add many more. The additions that Moses added would only be in effect until the coming of the Messiah.

Levi handed down the office of high priest to his son Kohath. Kohath instructed his children to observe all the laws of the priesthood and guard all of the testaments of their fathers which he had received from his father, Levi.

> "You must keep the priesthood in every way that I have commanded you... Amram, my son, I command you and your descendants... given to Levi my father, which he in turn gave to me along with all my writings as witness. You must take care of them. They are for you and your descendants and in them is great worth. It is important that they be carried on with you." *Testament of Kohath*

Kohath turned the priesthood over to his son Amram, with the instructions and records. According to the *Testament of Amram*, he left his wife and family in Egypt to go built the sepulchers of his fathers in the cave of Machpelah in Canaan. While there, a war broke out and because of it, he

The Order of Levi

was trapped and could not get back to his family for forty-one years! When Amram was finally able to be reunited with his family, Moses had already been banished from Egypt. Amram turned over the priesthood and records to Aaron his firstborn, Moses' brother. They waited for the fulfillment of the prophecy God gave to Abraham. They waited for the end of the 430 years when God would deliver them from Egypt.

God sent Aaron visions about their deliverance and the coming of the Messiah. See the section in *Melchizedekian Prophecy* for a full study in these prophecies.

The year of the Exodus, 2448 AM, God commanded that high priests of Israel were to come only from the line of Aaron.

The high priests from the Exodus to the time of King Solomon were Aaron, Eleazar, Phinehas, Abishua, Bukki, Uzzi, Eli, Ahitub, Ahijah, Ahimelech, and Abiathar. In the days of King Solomon, a conspiracy formed against Solomon. The high priest, Abiathar, sided against Solomon. Around 900 BC, Solomon deposed Abiathar and replaced him with a godly Levite descendant of Aaron named Zadok.

From this time on, only descendants of Zadok were allowed to be high priests. Legitimate Israeli kings could only come through the line of Judah, but later this lineage was narrowed to the line of David, a descendant of Judah. In the same way, a high priest had to be of the lineage of

Ancient Order of Melchizedek

Levi, but in time it was narrowed to the lineage of Aaron, a descendant of Levi, and finally narrowed again to a descendant of Aaron, namely Zadok. The book of Ezekiel says in the millennial reign there will be priests in the Temple that are only from the line of Zadok.

"It shall be for the priests that are sanctified of the sons of Zadok; which have kept My charge, which went not astray when the children of Israel went astray, as the Levites went astray." *Ezekiel 48:11*

The Zadok line of high priests that extended from Zadok to the Babylonian captivity were: Ahimaaz, Azariah, Johnan, Azatiah, Amaria, Ahitub II, Zadok II, Shallum, Hilkiah, Azariah IV, Seraiah, and Jehozadak. After returning from the Babylonian captivity, the Zadok line started with Joshua the son of Jehozadak. Around 175 BC a rebellion occurred that deposed the godly line of Zadok. The priests after the return from Babylon were: Joshua, Joiakim, Eliashib, Joiada, Johanan, Jaddua, Onias I, Simon I, Eleazar, Manasseh, Onias II, Simon II, Onias III, Onaias IV, and Jason.

Most of us remember Antiochus Epiphanes, who persecuted the Jews. He killed all those who refused to live a Grecian lifestyle. They could not study the Bible, practice circumcision, or do Jewish sacrifices. The Jerusalem temple was desolated with idols and Jews were forced to sacrifice to pagan gods or be put to death. The Zadok priests refused to obey, and the assassination of Zadok priests began.

The Order of Levi

The Zadok priests knew of the apostasy that was to come, and under inspiration of the Holy Spirit, took the temple library to Qumran. There the Lord protected them, and they prepared the hearts of the people for the coming of the Messiah. They did this as best as they could in the midst of a growing apostasy in the Sanhedrin, and in the Pharisee and Sadducee parties.

The Dead Sea Scrolls found in Qumran and its surrounding caves are the legacy of the Zadok priests with a complete history from their point of view.

The community in Qumran called themselves "Yahad." This is a contraction of two Hebrew words. "Yah" is the name of God and "ehad" means "one" in the sense of one group of brothers. So, the name "Yahad" literally means unity in the Spirit of God. They believed they were led directly by the Holy Spirit, so they truly were "one in the Spirit."

Their major center of ritual that we call Qumran, they called New Damascus. We learn this in the Damascus documents. Their name "Damascus" is made up of two Hebrew words; "dam" meaning blood and "Masheq" meaning "heir" or "stronghold." Look this up in Strong's concordance. "Dam" is H1818 and "mashaq" is H4944. New Damascus was the stronghold of the ancient ways and those loyal to the true blood heir, the coming Messiah.

Ancient Order of Melchizedek

Incidentally, the term "Melchizedek" translates out to mean King (Melech) of Righteousness (Zedeq) but it could also be translated as the "King of the Zadok priests!"

Jesus and John the Baptist

We have seen from various ancient records the progression of the Melchizedekian priests and the School of the Prophets from Adam down to Jacob, who, under inspiration of the Holy Spirit, broke up the Melchizedekian priesthood into three separate offices. These were king, prophet, and priest. The Gospel of Matthew reveals the genealogical record of Jesus Christ. Matthew begins with Abraham, Isaac, and Jacob. We know Jacob split up the Melchizedekian priesthood and thereby creating the line of kings from Judah and the priestly line from Levi. Matthew clearly shows Jesus as a direct biological descendant of Judah and therefore heir to the throne of David and destined to be king of Israel.

"The book of the generation of Jesus Christ, the son of David, the son of Abraham. Abraham begat Isaac; and Isaac begat Jacob; and Jacob begat Judas and his brethren; And Judas begat Phares and Zara of Thamar; and Phares begat Esrom; and Esrom begat Aram; And Aram begat Aminadab; and Aminadab begat Naasson; and Naasson begat Salmon; And Salmon begat Booz of Rachab; and Booz begat Obed of Ruth; and Obed begat Jesse; And Jesse begat David the king; and David the king begat Solomon of her that had been the wife of Urias; And Solomon begat Roboam; and Roboam begat Abia; and Abia begat Asa; And Asa begat Josaphat; and Josaphat

Ancient Order of Melchizedek

begat Joram; and Joram begat Ozias; And Ozias begat Joatham; and Joatham begat Achaz; and Achaz begat Ezekias; And Ezekias begat Manasses; and Manasses begat Amon; and Amon begat Josias; And Josias begat Jechonias and his brethren, about the time they were carried away to Babylon: And after they were brought to Babylon, Jechonias begat Salathiel; and Salathiel begat Zorobabel; And Zorobabel begat Abiud; and Abiud begat Eliakim; and Eliakim begat Azor; And Azor begat Sadoc; and Sadoc begat Achim; and Achim begat Eliud; And Eliud begat Eleazar; and Eleazar begat Matthan; and Matthan begat Jacob; And Jacob begat Joseph the husband of Mary, of whom was born Jesus, who is called Christ." *Matthew 1:1-16*

But what about the priestly lines and the School of the Prophets? God has graciously preserved that record too. The *Ante-Nicene Fathers* is a ten-volume work comprising what was written about the church and its history from AD 32 to AD 325. In this set there exists a record entitled "Hippolytus' *Fragments on the Pentateuch*." No one really realized what this document was, until after some of the Dead Sea Scrolls told of the ancient histories and apostasies. It is a complete record of the priestly prophetic line from the time of Moses down to the Church Age. To bridge the gap, remember that Jacob made Levi the priest. Levi handed that down to his son Kohath, who handed it to his son Amram. Amram was the father of Moses and Aaron. Hippolytus does not give the history of the kings of Israel nor high priests of Israel, but rather the prophetic line

Jesus and John the Baptist

that ran the School of the Prophets, from Moses to John the Baptist. Here is that record:

> "These following are the names of the teachers who handed down the Law in continuous succession after Moses the prophet, until the advent of Messiah: God delivered the most excellent Law into the hands of Moses the prophet, the son of Amram."
> *Hippolytus' Fragments on the Pentateuch*

He then gives a long line of their names:

1. Moses
2. Joshua
3. Othniel
4. Jehud
5. Shamgar
6. Baruk
7. Gideon
8. Abimelech
9. Taleg
10. Babin
11. Jephthah
12. Ephran
13. Elul
14. Abdon
15. Samson
16. Elkanah (father of Samuel the prophet)
17. Eli the priest
18. Samuel the prophet
19. Nathan the prophet

Ancient Order of Melchizedek

20. Gad the prophet,
21. Shemaiah the teacher
22. Iddo the teacher
23. Ahijah the Shilonite
24. Abihu
25. Elijah the prophet
26. Elisha the prophet
27. Micah the prophet
28. Abdiahu
29. Jehuda
30. Zacharias the teacher
31. Esaia the prophet (the son of Amos)
32. Jeremiah the prophet
33. Ezekiel
34. Hosea the prophet (the son of Bazi)
35. Joel the prophet
36. Amos the prophet
37. Obadiah
38. Jonan the prophet (son of Mathi, the son of Armelah, who was the brother of Elias the prophet)
39. Micha the Morasthite
40. Nachum the Alcusite
41. Habakkuk the prophet
42. Zephaniah the prophet
43. Haggai the prophet
44. Zechariah the prophet (the son of Bershia)
45. Malachi
46. Ezra the teacher
47. Shamai the chief priest
48. Jaduah

Jesus and John the Baptist

49. Samean
50. Antigonus
51. Joseph (son of Johezer) and Joseph (the son of Gjuchanan)
52. Jehosua (son of Barachia)
53. Nathan the Arbelite
54. Simeon (elder son of Shebach. This is the Simeon who held the Messiah in his arms.)
55. Jehuda
56. Zechariah the priest (father of John the Baptist)
57. Joseph (a teacher of the tribe of Levi)
58. Annas and Caiaphas

Hippolytus goes on to say:

"Joseph delivered it to Annas and Caiaphas. Moreover, from them were taken away the priestly, and kingly, and prophetic offices. These were teachers at the advent of Messiah; and they were both priests of the children of Israel. Therefore, the whole number of venerable and honorable priests put in trust of this most excellent law was fifty-six, Annas and Caiaphas being excepted. And those are they who delivered it in the last days to the state of the children of Israel; nor did there arise any priests after them. This is the account of what took place with regard to the most excellent Law."

Hippolytus' Fragments on the Pentateuch

What is the most interesting thing to note about this text is that Annas and Caiaphas were evil, but had the title of chief

Ancient Order of Melchizedek

priest and leader of the School of the Prophets. In reality, if they became apostate, then by Mosaic Law, the true leader would be the last in succession. So, the head of the School of the Prophets in Qumran would fall back to this Joseph the Levite. If he died without having any children, it would revert back to the previous leader who would be Zechariah the priest, and his firstborn son was John the Baptist.

In the writings of church father Clement, a disciple of the apostle Peter, there exists a historical record of how Simon Magus, of Acts 8:9-25, became the father of the Gnostic heretics. This is recorded in the *Clement's Homilies 2.23-24* and the *Recognitions of Clement 1.54; 2.8,11*. At the beginning of this narrative, Clement explains that Simon was originally a disciple of John the Baptist in his school. Clement says,

> "There was one John, a day-baptist, who was the forerunner of our Lord Jesus; and as the Lord had twelve apostles, bearing the number of the twelve months of the sun, so also he, John, had thirty chief men, fulfilling the number of days in a month, in which number was a certain woman called Helena, that not even this might be without a dispensational significance." *Clement's Homilies 2.23*

In keeping with the solar Dead Sea Scroll calendar, the higher teaching groups / Sanhedrin consisted of twelve and the lower teaching groups / Sanhedrin consisted of thirty. In this way the Essenes demonstrated the God-ordained use

Jesus and John the Baptist

of the solar calendar and not the corrupted Pharisee / Sadducee lunar calendar. See *Ancient Dead Sea Scroll Calendar* by this author. In the Essene pattern, Jesus the Messiah had twelve disciples and John the Baptist, the lower teacher, had thirty disciples. This alone shows a strong Essene connection to Jesus Christ and John the Baptist, but there is more.

Josephus records that there were two groups of Essenes, the Qumran Essenes (godly Jews who kept the scrolls and studied the prophecies) and the Egyptian Essenes (who despised prophecy, and instead practiced a system of magic which was forbidden to Jews in Israel). Much like today, Christian denominations and cults both claim the name of "Christian."

Clement further says that Simon fell away from the study of the Messianic prophecies and, not wanting to wait on the Lord, left John's school to travel to Egypt to study magic with the Egyptian Essenes. Upon Simon's return from Egypt, he found John was dead, the Messiah had come, and many of the old students were now following Jesus as the true Messiah. Some of John's school did not accept Jesus as Messiah and those were led by an old disciple of John named Dositheus.

> "But of these thirty, the first and the most esteemed by John was Simon; and the reason of his not being chief after the death of John was as follows: He [Simon Magus] being absent in Egypt for the practice of magic, and John being killed, Dositheus desiring

the leadership, falsely gave out that Simon was dead, and succeeded to the seat. But Simon, returning not long after, and strenuously holding by the place as his own, when he met with Dositheus did not demand the place, knowing that a man who has attained power beyond his expectations cannot be removed from it. Wherefore with pretended friendship he gives himself for a while to the second place, under Dositheus. But taking his place after a few days among the thirty fellow-disciples, he began to malign Dositheus as not delivering the instructions correctly..." *Clement's Homilies 2.24*

Just like the cults of today, they come into a church claiming they believe the same doctrine and just want to be friends and study under the current pastor, all the while they intend to underhandedly cause division in the church. Simon caused doubt and division and then used his magic tricks to deceive. Eventually all the group and Dositheus himself fell for Simon's lies. Clement finished the narrative by saying,

"he raised Simon to his own place of repute; and thus, not many days after, Dositheus himself, while he (Simon) stood, fell down and died."
Clement's Homilies 2.24

"some even of the disciples of John, who seemed to be great ones, have separated themselves from the people, and proclaimed their own master as the Christ." *Recognitions of Clement 1.54*

Jesus and John the Baptist

John the Baptist was baptizing in the Jordan river just eight miles from where Qumran was at that time. There is a Dead Sea Scroll called the Community Rule which records not only how to become an Essene, but how they started. The Community Rule says when the apostasy hit, the Holy Spirit spoke to their leaders, the Zadok priests, instructing them to move out of Jerusalem into the wilderness taking the temple library with them. They said that the Holy Spirit told them one of their order would fulfill the prophecy of Isaiah which says,

> "The voice of him that crieth in the wilderness, Prepare ye the way of the LORD, make straight in the desert a highway for our God. Every valley shall be exalted, and every mountain and hill shall be made low: and the crooked shall be made straight, and the rough places plain: And the glory of the LORD shall be revealed, and all flesh shall see it together: for the mouth of the LORD hath spoken it." *Isaiah 40:3-5*

In their mind the Essene order would keep proper doctrine and wait for the coming of the Messiah. When He came, He would destroy the Pharisees and Sadducees and end the corrupt Levitical priesthood by establishing a new Melchizedekian order and usher in a new age called the Age of Grace. I have more on this in the section, *Melchizedekian Prophecy*. The Community Rule says,

> "When these join the [Essene] community in Israel and comply with the community rules, they are to separate themselves from the men of sin and dwell in

Ancient Order of Melchizedek

> the desert in order to 'open His path.' As it is written 'The voice crying in the wilderness, Prepare the way of the LORD, make a straight highway in the desert for our God. [Isaiah 40:3]'"
> *Community Rule, col. 8*

The Gospel of John records John the Baptist's answer to the Pharisee's question of who he was,

> "Then they said to him, 'Who are you so that we may give an answer to those who sent us? What do you say of yourself?' He said, 'I am "the voice of one crying in the wilderness: Make straight the way of the Lord," as the prophet Isaiah said.'"
> *John 1:22-23 MKJV*

We know Jesus the Messiah never committed any sin. So why did John baptize Jesus? John was baptizing Him into the priesthood. If Jesus was the Messiah born of the kingly lineage of David, and John baptized Him into the Priesthood, and God blessed it by sending the Holy Spirit to make Him a prophet, it would mean the reestablishing of the ancient Melchizedekian priesthood. Scripture records,

> "Then cometh Jesus from Galilee to Jordan unto John, to be baptized of him. But John forbad Him, saying, I have need to be baptized of Thee, and comest Thou to me? And Jesus answering said unto him, Suffer it to be so now: for thus it becometh us to fulfil all righteousness. Then he suffered Him. And

Jesus and John the Baptist

Jesus, when He was baptized, went up straightway out of the water: and, lo, the heavens were opened unto Him, and He saw the Spirit of God descending like a dove, and lighting upon Him: And lo a voice from heaven, saying, This is My beloved Son, in whom I am well pleased." *Matthew 3:13-17*

John knew that Jesus was sinless, which is why he said, "I have need to be baptized of Thee, and comest Thou to me?" Jesus needed John to baptize Him into the priesthood to reestablish the Melchizedekian priesthood, which would make it possible for Jesus to "fulfill all righteousness."

We do not see the School of the Prophets again until the book of Acts when the school's leader came down from Antioch with some of his students to give a prophecy to the apostle Paul.

"And in these days came prophets from Jerusalem unto Antioch. And there stood up one of them named Agabus, and signified by the Spirit that there should be great dearth throughout all the world: which came to pass in the days of Claudius Caesar."
Acts 11:27-28

"And as we tarried there many days, there came down from Judaea a certain prophet, named Agabus. And when he was come unto us, he took Paul's girdle, and bound his own hands and feet, and said, Thus saith the Holy Ghost, So shall the Jews at Jerusalem

Ancient Order of Melchizedek

bind the man that owneth this girdle, and shall deliver him into the hands of the Gentiles." *Acts 21:10-11*

This makes John the Baptist the leader of the School of the Prophets and an Essene. This means he was the only one with the authority to baptize Jesus into the priesthood! The ancient church fathers record the successors to Agabus and the School, but this will suffice for now.

Church father Hippolytus concludes his narrative by describing that Titus destroyed the Jerusalem temple and the nation of Israel was dissolved, all because of the apostasy of the Sadducees and Pharisees.

"And after the ascension of Christ into heaven, came King Titus, son of Vespasian king of Rome, to Jerusalem, and besieged and took it. And he destroyed the edifice of the second house, which the children of Israel had built. Titus the king destroyed the house of the sanctuary, and slew all the Jews who were in it, and bathed Zion in their blood. And after that deportation the Jews were scattered abroad in slavery. Nor did they assemble any more in the city of Jerusalem, nor is there hope anywhere of their returning. Jerusalem was laid waste because Shemaia and Antalia (Abtalion) perverted the law."
Hippolytus' *Fragments on the Pentateuch*

Conclusion

Church father Hippolytus gives the lineage of the leader of the School of the Prophets from the time of Moses down to John the Baptist. We have seen the biblical record of Jesus being born of the lineage of King David, being baptized into the priesthood by John the Baptist, the leader in the Zadok / Essene movement, and the Holy Spirit descending on Jesus like a dove adding the spirit of prophecy to the event. Thus, Jesus was then made priest, king, and prophet. The Melchizedekian priesthood that was divided by Jacob was now restored in Jesus Christ.

Ancient Order of Melchizedek

Melchizedekian Theology

Melchizedek in the Bible

In this section on Melchizedekian theology, we turn to Jesus, Moses, King David, and the apostles Paul and Peter, to carefully learn what they taught about the Messiah's priesthood and covenant, and how that relates to the Melchizedekian priesthood.

First, we will look at how Paul and Jesus used Psalm 110 to teach about the Messiah's new priesthood.

Second, we will look at the theology of the apostle Paul about the Melchizedekian priesthood in Hebrews 5 through Hebrews 8.

Lastly, we will tie all of this together by looking at teachings from the apostles Peter, John, and Paul.

Psalm 110

King David wrote Psalm 110 about 1000 BC. It is about the coming Messiah.

Modern Judaism teaches that Psalm 110 refers to Genesis 14:17-24, where a man named Melchizedek blessed Abraham and prophetically transferred the office of priest to Abraham's descendant Aaron. So, in their mind there is no difference between a Melchizedekian priest and an Aaronic priest. They are one and the same. They also believe that Psalm 110 teaches that the priesthood of Aaron is eternal. All of this is a modern-day error and stems from a teaching in *The Zohar,* a Kabalistic book written in the middle ages.

In the first century AD, all three sects of Jews, the Sadducees, the Pharisees, and the Essenes, believed that this text referred to the promised Messiah. One of the titles for the Messiah was "Son of David." There are many places throughout the Gospels where the people called Jesus the "Son of David." That was the people's way of acknowledging that they believed that Jesus was indeed the promised Messiah. A few references where people ask for mercy and healing from Jesus by calling Him the "Son of David" are: Matthew 9:27; 15:22; 20:30; 21:9; 21:15; 22:42; Mark 10:47-48; 12:35; Luke 18:38-39.

Ancient Order of Melchizedek

The Essenes still believed that the Messiah would be God incarnate, but the Pharisees and Sadducees had started teaching that the Messiah would be just a man sent by God to win a war. When the Pharisees were giving Jesus trouble, He decided to ask them a question from Psalm 110 that would silence them.

> "While the Pharisees were gathered together, Jesus asked them, saying, What think ye of Christ? whose son is He? They say unto Him, The Son of David. He saith unto them, How then doth David in spirit call Him Lord, saying, The LORD said unto my Lord, Sit Thou on My right hand, till I make Thine enemies Thy footstool? If David then call Him Lord, how is He his son? And no man was able to answer Him a word, neither durst any man from that day forth ask Him any more questions." *Matthew 22:41-46*

The Gospel of Mark gives the same record but reveals that the "scribes," or Essenes, were known to teach that the Messiah was God incarnate. The term "scribe" is used for Essenes when referring to those who kept the written records of the temple library. Sometimes it also refers to those who copied court documents regardless of affiliation. Mark is referring to those who kept the temple scrolls; therefore, these scribes were Essenes.

> "And Jesus answered and said, while He taught in the temple, How say the scribes that Christ is the Son of David? For David himself said by the Holy Ghost, The LORD said to my Lord, Sit Thou on My right

Psalm 110

hand, till I make Thine enemies Thy footstool. David therefore himself calleth Him Lord; and whence is He then his son? And the common people heard Him gladly." *Mark 12:35-37*

An Essene would have answered correctly by saying the Christ, or Messiah, is a direct descendant of King David and therefore would be subject to His father King David, but since the Messiah is God incarnate, David would call Him "Lord," instead of the other way around. The Pharisees, who wanted to make the Christ a mere man, couldn't answer this question without causing themselves even more disgrace in the eyes of the people. They refused to answer the question.

This proves that all three sects knew this Psalm of David refers to the coming Messiah and not Aaron. They also knew that there is a difference between the two orders of priests. The two priesthoods were not the same. With this in mind let us look at Psalm 110 closely,

> "A Psalm of David. The LORD said unto my Lord, Sit Thou at My right hand, until I make Thine enemies Thy footstool. The LORD shall send the rod of Thy strength out of Zion: rule Thou in the midst of Thine enemies. Thy people shall be willing in the day of Thy power, in the beauties of holiness from the womb of the morning: Thou hast the dew of Thy youth. The LORD hath sworn, and will not repent, Thou art a priest for ever after the order of Melchizedek. The Lord at Thy right hand shall strike

Ancient Order of Melchizedek

through kings in the day of His wrath. He shall judge among the heathen, He shall fill the places with the dead bodies; He shall wound the heads over many countries. He shall drink of the brook in the way: therefore shall He lift up the head." *Psalms 110:1-7*

So, the Messiah is the "Son of David." David knows "the LORD," is God the Father, and that the Messiah is his "Lord," or God incarnate. So how does this God-man, born king of the lineage of David save us by a priestly action? The Law of Moses forbids anyone not of the lineage of Levi to be made a Levitical priest. God the Father swears an oath that cannot be broken, the Messiah will be a priest of the Order of Melchizedek, not of the Order of Levi.

The apostle Paul used Psalm 110 several times in his teaching about Jesus and the Melchizedekian order in the book of Hebrews.

The Book of Hebrews

The apostle Paul teaches on the Melchizedekian order in several chapters in the book of Hebrews. First let us outline the book of Hebrews to see why Paul talks about the order so much.

Paul was writing to the Hebrew priests who were serving in the temple. Some were thinking about accepting Jesus as Messiah and others basically believed, but did not want to stop being priests. The temple would be destroyed within the next twenty years.

The book of Hebrews is divided into two sections. Chapters one through ten deal with the theology of Jesus Christ. Chapters eleven through thirteen deal with practical matters of the Christian walk.

In each chapter of the first section of the book of Hebrews, the apostle Paul describes how Jesus is superior to everything held dear to the Jews. Jesus is the Messiah, and all rituals and Mosaic Laws were types and shadows to point to Him. He fulfilled everything they pointed to. All the temple priests needed to do would be to accept the Messiah now before it was too late.

Ancient Order of Melchizedek

Here is an outline of the chapters of the first section.

1. Jesus is superior to all the prophets and angels.
2. Jesus is superior to all men.
3. Jesus is superior to Moses.
4. Jesus brings a rest superior to the Sabbath.
5. Jesus is superior to the Levitical priesthood.
6. Paul warns not to reject the Messiah.
7. Jesus is of the Order of Melchizedekian priests.
8. Jesus brings a superior new covenant.
9. The superiority of the heavenly tabernacle and new covenant is compared to the earthly Mosaic tabernacle and the old Mosaic covenant.
10. Jesus' one-time sacrifice is superior to the sacrifices of all the bulls and goats.

Hebrews 5

In this first part of Hebrews 5, Paul begins teaching about the priesthood of Jesus Christ. Paul's first point is that all priests are taken from men to intercede between men and God. There are no angel priests, just human priests. Human priests must offer sacrifice for themselves first, in order to be able to offer sacrifice on the behalf of others.

> "For every high priest taken from among men is ordained for men in things pertaining to God, that he may offer both gifts and sacrifices for sins: Who can have compassion on the ignorant, and on them that are out of the way; for that he himself also is compassed with infirmity. And by reason hereof he ought, as for the people, so also for himself, to offer for sins." *Hebrews 5:1-3*

Paul's second point is that only God can ordain a priest. God spoke and ordained Aaron to be the first high priest of the Aaronic priesthood.

> "And no man taketh this honour unto himself, but he that is called of God, as was Aaron." *Hebrews 5:4*

In the same way, God spoke and ordained Jesus to be a high priest. To prove Jesus is a priest ordained by God and not by men, Paul quotes two biblical passages. The first is from Psalm 2.

Ancient Order of Melchizedek

Paul quotes part of Psalm 2 to remind them that the prophecy shows their rulers would be enraged against Him and seek to kill Him. This is exactly what happened to Jesus.

> "Why do the heathen rage, and the people imagine a vain thing? The kings of the earth set themselves, and the rulers take counsel together, against the LORD, and against His anointed [Messiah]… I will declare the decree: the LORD hath said unto Me, Thou art My Son; this day have I begotten Thee."
> *Psalms 2:1-2, 7*

The apostle Paul is quoting this not only to prove Jesus was to be persecuted, but also to show when He was to be ordained as a priest. It was when the Father would say "Thou art My Son, today have I begotten Thee."

> "So also Christ glorified not Himself to be made an high priest; but He that said unto Him, Thou art My Son, today have I begotten Thee." *Hebrews 5:5*

Jesus was from the tribe of Judah, not Levi, so it was illegal for Him to be ordained as a Levitical priest. So, Paul immediately reminds them that the prophecy in Psalm 110 dictated that the Messiah was to be a priest of a *different* order. He was to be a Melchizedekian priest.

> "As He saith also in another place, Thou art a priest for ever after the order of Melchisedec."
> *Hebrews 5:6*

Hebrews 5

The second passage quoted is from Psalm 110.

> "The LORD hath sworn, and will not repent, Thou art a priest for ever after the order of Melchizedek." *Psalms 110:4*

Jesus was perfect so He did not have to offer anything for Himself. Paul then explains that the Messiah, the new Melchizedekian priest, was to offer Himself for the sins of His people. This would once and for all time bring an "eternal salvation."

> "Who in the days of His flesh, when He had offered up prayers and supplications with strong crying and tears unto Him that was able to save Him from death, and was heard in that He feared; Though He were a Son, yet learned He obedience by the things which He suffered; And being made perfect, He became the author of eternal salvation unto all them that obey Him; Called of God an high priest after the order of Melchisedec." *Hebrews 5:7-10*

When did God ordain Jesus as high priest? When He said, "Thou art My Son; this day have I begotten Thee." We see in Matthew 3 and Mark 1, that this happened when John the Baptist baptized Jesus into the priesthood.

> "Then cometh Jesus from Galilee to Jordan unto John, to be baptized of him. But John forbad Him, saying, I have need to be baptized of Thee, and comest Thou to me? And Jesus answering said unto

him, Suffer it to be so now: for thus it becometh us to fulfil all righteousness. Then he suffered Him. And Jesus, when He was baptized, went up straightway out of the water: and, lo, the heavens were opened unto Him, and He saw the Spirit of God descending like a dove, and lighting upon Him: And lo a voice from heaven, saying, This is My beloved Son, in whom I am well pleased." *Matthew 3:13-17*

The apostle Paul ends the fifth chapter of Hebrews by saying,

"Of whom we have many things to say, and hard to be uttered, seeing ye are dull of hearing. For when for the time ye ought to be teachers, ye have need that one teach you again which be the first principles of the oracles of God; and are become such as have need of milk, and not of strong meat. For every one that useth milk is unskilful in the word of righteousness: for he is a babe. But strong meat belongeth to them that are of full age, even those who by reason of use have their senses exercised to discern both good and evil." *Hebrews 5:11-14*

Notice that there are many things Paul could teach them about Jesus and the Melchizedekian priesthood, but the Pharisaical priests were "dull of hearing." The Hebrew idiom "dull of hearing" does not mean they were stupid, that they could not understand plain speech. It means obstinate. If Paul would have just spelled it out clearly, they would have rejected his teaching as "that old Essene garbage." So, Paul had to take it slowly and prove point by point from the only writing both he and the Pharisees accepted, the Torah.

Conclusion

In Hebrews 5 the apostle Paul states that Jesus is the Messiah, and that He was ordained into the priesthood by God the Father. Jesus is not a Levitical priest, but a priest of the Order of Melchizedek. Jesus was ordained into this priesthood when John the Baptist baptized Him. Paul said there was a lot more he could tell us about the Melchizedekian order, but the Pharisees would refuse to listen to him if he was too direct with them. Thanks to the Dead Sea Scrolls, we now know a lot more of what Paul could have recorded in the book of Hebrews.

Hebrews 6

In chapter 6 of the book of Hebrews, Paul continues his thought of not obsessing about small points of the Mosaic Law, but rather to go on to a perfect understanding of the Messiah and His new priesthood.

> "Therefore leaving the principles of the doctrine of Christ, let us go on unto perfection; not laying again the foundation of repentance from dead works, and of faith toward God, Of the doctrine of baptisms, and of laying on of hands, and of resurrection of the dead, and of eternal judgment. And this will we do, if God permit." *Hebrews 6:1-3*

Paul then gives a warning not to reject the Messiah and His Melchizedekian priesthood.

> "For it is impossible for those who were once enlightened, and have tasted of the heavenly gift, and were made partakers of the Holy Ghost, And have tasted the good word of God, and the powers of the world to come, If they shall fall away, to renew them again unto repentance; seeing they crucify to themselves the Son of God afresh, and put Him to an open shame. For the earth which drinketh in the rain that cometh oft upon it, and bringeth forth herbs meet for them by whom it is dressed, receiveth blessing from God: But that which beareth thorns and briers

is rejected, and is nigh unto cursing; whose end is to be burned." *Hebrews 6:4-8*

These temple priests were there. They saw how the Messiah fulfilled these prophecies. They should not, they could not, in good conscience, forget those things and just go back to doing the daily temple sacrifices. Paul warned that the end of those who reject Messiah is to be burned. When Paul wrote the Book of Hebrews, there were only about fifteen years left before the great temple in Jerusalem would be burned. Those who rejected the Messiah and held to the old ways and fought the Romans were either killed or taken into captivity. Paul is warning them they only have a few years to make a decision or it will be made for them. Today we should take to heart that same warning. We only have a few years before the tribulation starts. We all must make a decision to accept the Messiah's free gift of salvation while we are still able to do so.

Paul then pleaded with them to not allow Satan to cloud their minds. They should not forget their commitment to the Messiah. Their lives depended on it.

> "But, beloved, we are persuaded better things of you, and things that accompany salvation, though we thus speak. For God is not unrighteous to forget your work and labour of love, which ye have shewed toward His name, in that ye have ministered to the saints, and do minister. And we desire that every one of you do shew the same diligence to the full assurance of hope unto the end: That ye be not

Ancient Order of Melchizedek

slothful, but followers of them who through faith and patience inherit the promises." *Hebrews 6:9-12*

Paul then reminded them God swore an oath that the nation of Israel would exist. Likewise, He swore an oath that the Messiah would be a Melchizedekian priest. Neither of these oaths of God can be changed.

"For when God made promise to Abraham, because He could swear by no greater, He sware by Himself, Saying, Surely blessing I will bless thee, and multiplying I will multiply thee. And so, after he had patiently endured, he obtained the promise. For men verily swear by the greater: and an oath for confirmation is to them an end of all strife. Wherein God, willing more abundantly to shew unto the heirs of promise the immutability of His counsel, confirmed it by an oath: That by two immutable things, in which it was impossible for God to lie, we might have a strong consolation, who have fled for refuge to lay hold upon the hope set before us: Which hope we have as an anchor of the soul, both sure and steadfast, and which entereth into that within the veil; Whither the forerunner is for us entered, even Jesus, made an high priest for ever after the order of Melchisedec." *Hebrews 6:13-20*

When God wants you to know He is going to do something, that it is certain, and there is absolutely no way that God's decree will be stopped, He swears an oath. Paul gives the example that God swore an oath to Abraham that the nation of Israel would exist. The priests reading this New Testament epistle are living proof that that promise was fulfilled. In the same way, if God swore an oath that Jesus would be made a high priest after the Order of Melchizedek, it must be so, or God would be a liar. If this is true, His new priesthood has replaced the Aaronic priesthood in the same way that the Zadok priests said it would happen.

Conclusion
In chapter 6 of Hebrews, Paul teaches us that we should not be caught up in points of the Mosaic Law, but be focused on more important things, like the prophecies about the Messiah, His new covenant and priesthood. Never let some point of the Law keep you away from the Messiah.

Hebrews 7

Hebrews 7 is the chapter we want to take very slowly. First Paul says,

> "For this Melchisedec, king of Salem, priest of the most high God, who met Abraham returning from the slaughter of the kings, and blessed him; To whom also Abraham gave a tenth part of all; first being by interpretation King of righteousness, and after that also King of Salem, which is, King of peace;" *Hebrews 7:1-2*

If Paul would have been speaking of the man "Levi" it would be spelled l-e-v-i. If he would have been speaking of a Levite priest, the Hebrew would still be spelled l-e-v-i. In Hebrew, a "y" sound is added to the end of the name of a nation like "Israel" to make it "Israeli." So, the addition to the word changes it from the name of the *man*, Israel, to the name of the *people*, Israeli. This chapter is going to be concentrating on the office of Melchizedek not any one person who held that office.

With this in mind, verse 1 is usually interpreted as "this man who was named Melchizedek was…" instead of the way the context suggests, which is "this Melchizedekian priest was…" Either way it is referring to the one who blessed Abraham in Genesis 14:17-24. But we will see why this has to be interpreted as "this Melchizedekian priest."

Hebrews 7

Paul gives the definition of what the word "Melchizedek" means. It is two Hebrew words added together to create the title of a priesthood. The word "Melech" means king and the word "Zedek" means righteous or righteousness. So, Melchizedek means "King of Righteousness." Alternatively, it *could* be translated as King of the Zadok priests.

The priest who blessed Abraham was the king of Salem. The word "Salem" is a derivative of "shalom" which means "peace" in Hebrew. Salem was a small area like a suburb in Jerusalem, where Shem and Eber had their School of the Prophets. The name later came to mean the whole area. Later still, when King David took over the city, it was renamed Jerusalem.

There is much confusion about verse 3. Most read it as "the man Melchizedek was without father or mother…" which would mean he was not human. This is why many have taught that this refers to a Christophany, a pre-incarnate appearance of Jesus Christ. Christophanies are recorded as happening in other places in the Old Testament. But this is not one of them. Let us read it very carefully.

> "Without father, without mother, without descent, having neither beginning of days, nor end of life; but made like unto the Son of God; abideth a priest continually." *Hebrews 7:3*

Ancient Order of Melchizedek

If we understand that Paul is speaking about the *order* of Melchizedek contrasted with the *order* of Levi, it suddenly makes sense.

To be a Levitical priest one had to be not only a Jew (no Gentiles allowed), but one had to be a direct descendant of Levi (no other tribes allowed). This applies to both the mother and the father.

> "Bring the tribe of Levi near, and present them before Aaron the priest, that they may minister unto him. And they shall keep his charge, and the charge of the whole congregation before the tabernacle of the congregation, to do the service of the tabernacle." *Numbers 3:6-7*

The Levite must start apprenticing at the age of twenty, start actually performing his duties as priest by the age of twenty-five, and there was a mandatory retirement at the age of fifty.

> "This is it that belongeth unto the Levites: from twenty and five years old and upward they shall go in to wait upon the service of the tabernacle of the congregation: And from the age of fifty years they shall cease waiting upon the service thereof, and shall serve no more." *Numbers 8:24-25*

In contrast, the superior Melchizedekian priesthood does not have any requirement of being from a certain tribe of Israel. A Melchizedekian priest starts performing his duties

Hebrews 7

as a priest whenever the last high priest, or God, ordains him. Unlike the Levitical priesthood, the Melchizedekian priesthood is only stopped by death. There is no mandatory retirement. So, let's put these verses together with the added information from the book of Numbers.

"For this <u>Melchisedekian priest</u>, king of Salem, priest of the most high God, who met Abraham returning from the slaughter of the kings, and <u>blessed and ordained</u> him; To whom also Abraham gave a tenth part of all; <u>the priesthood's name is</u> first being by interpretation King of righteousness, and after that also King of Salem, which is, King of peace; <u>this superior priesthood is</u> without father, without mother, without descent, having neither beginning of days, nor end of life; <u>so unlike the order of Levi, the order of Melchizedek is</u> made like unto the Son of God; <u>the Melchizedekian order and the Messiah can both</u> abide as a priest continually, <u>the order of Levi cannot</u>." *Hebrews 7:1-3 paraphrased*

The apostle Paul then turns to another point proving the superiority of the priesthood of Jesus. Only the Levitical priesthood can collect tithes from the children of Israel. But Abraham paid tithes to his teacher / Melchizedekian priest when Levi had not yet been born. So, in a sense, Levi was paying tithes to the Melchizedekian priest. That should fully show its superiority.

"Now consider how great this man was, unto whom even the patriarch Abraham gave the tenth of the spoils. And verily they that are of the sons of Levi, who receive the office of the priesthood, have a commandment to take tithes of the people according to the law, that is, of their brethren, though they come out of the loins of Abraham: But he whose descent is not counted from them received tithes of Abraham, and blessed him that had the promises. And without all contradiction the less is blessed of the better. And here men that die receive tithes; but there he receiveth them, of whom it is witnessed that he liveth. And as I may so say, Levi also, who receiveth tithes, payed tithes in Abraham. For he was yet in the loins of his father, when Melchisedec met him." *Hebrews 7:4-10*

Notice also that verse 6 [below] says that the person who was the Melchizedekian priest who blessed Abraham did, indeed, have a genealogical descent. His descent was not after Levi, but was much older. So, we know Paul's point was to contrast the two different orders of priests.

"But he whose descent is not counted from them received tithes of Abraham, and blessed him that had the promises." *Hebrews 7:6*

Paul then asks the question [verse 11] why would God send the Messiah to be a priest but not of the Order of Aaron? The only answer could be that the Order of Aaron was not good enough. That order of priests, with its laws, cannot save. But the Messiah can.

Hebrews 7

"If therefore perfection were by the Levitical priesthood, (for under it the people received the law,) what further need was there that another priest should rise after the order of Melchisedec, and not be called after the order of Aaron?" *Hebrews 7:11*

Paul now gives a startling announcement, one that we need to grasp today. If there is a change in the priesthood, then there must also be a change in the priestly laws. Levitical priests must retire at fifty. The Melchizedekian priest does not have a mandatory retirement, and since the Messiah will never die, His priesthood is now eternal!

"For the priesthood being changed, there is made of necessity a change also of the law. For he of whom these things are spoken pertaineth to another tribe, of which no man gave attendance at the altar. For it is evident that our Lord sprang out of Juda; of which tribe Moses spake nothing concerning priesthood. And it is yet far more evident: for that after the similitude of Melchisedec there ariseth another priest, Who is made, not after the law of a carnal commandment, but after the power of an endless life. For he testifieth, Thou art a priest for ever after the order of Melchisedec." *Hebrews 7:12-17*

Many of our Hebrew Roots brothers want to be under the Mosaic Law, here referred to as the Levitical law. They believe Jesus just changed a few things here and there, but Paul makes it clear that we are in a whole different priesthood, with completely different laws and a

Ancient Order of Melchizedek

completely different covenant. When God swore the oath to make Jesus the Melchizedekian priest, He made it eternal. God swore it would be forever!

> "For there is verily a disannulling of the commandment going before for the weakness and unprofitableness thereof. For the law made nothing perfect, but the bringing in of a better hope did; by the which we draw nigh unto God. And inasmuch as not without an oath He was made priest: (For those priests were made without an oath; but this with an oath by Him that said unto Him, The Lord sware and will not repent, Thou art a priest for ever after the order of Melchisedec:)" *Hebrews 7:18-21*

Now we know how the priesthood of Jesus Christ is different from both the Melchizedekian and Aaronic priesthoods. Both had to hand the priesthood over to others, either because of mandatory retirement or because of death. Jesus is eternal and will never hand the priesthood over to another. It is our Lord and Savior, Jesus Christ, who truly makes the Melchizedekian priesthood superior to any other!

> "By so much was Jesus made a surety of a better testament. And they truly were many priests, because they were not suffered to continue by reason of death: But this man, because He continueth ever, hath an unchangeable priesthood. Wherefore He is able also to save them to the uttermost that come unto God by Him, seeing He ever liveth to make

intercession for them. For such an high priest became us, who is holy, harmless, undefiled, separate from sinners, and made higher than the heavens; Who needeth not daily, as those high priests, to offer up sacrifice, first for his own sins, and then for the people's: for this He did once, when He offered up Himself. For the law maketh men high priests which have infirmity; but the word of the oath, which was since the law, maketh the Son, who is consecrated for evermore." *Hebrews 7:22-28*

Conclusion
In this chapter we learned that Melchizedek was an order, not a person. Verse six says that the Melchizedekian priest that blessed Abraham did have a genealogical family tree (descent, father, and mother); he was just not a descendant of Levi. The priesthood of Levi was abolished and replaced by the Melchizedekian priesthood. This also makes a change in the law system and a change in the covenants.

Hebrews 8

Paul starts Hebrews 8 by summarizing his theology about the Messiah. From this point on Jesus is the only high priest. He will be the only high priest throughout eternity. Jesus serves His priestly duty in the real sanctuary in heaven. The earthly Mosaic tabernacle was just a copy or a type that symbolized the real one.

> "Now of the things which we have spoken this is the sum: We have such an high priest, who is set on the right hand of the throne of the Majesty in the heavens; A minister of the sanctuary, and of the true tabernacle, which the Lord pitched, and not man."
> *Hebrews 8:1-2*

Jesus offered Himself, not animals, for a sacrifice. All the temple ceremonies were simply rituals that pointed to what the Messiah would do to bring eternal salvation for all mankind.

> "For every high priest is ordained to offer gifts and sacrifices: wherefore it is of necessity that this man have somewhat also to offer. For if He were on earth, He should not be a priest, seeing that there are priests that offer gifts according to the law: Who serve unto the example and shadow of heavenly things, as Moses was admonished of God when he was about to make the tabernacle: for, See, saith He, that thou

make all things according to the pattern shewed to thee in the mount." *Hebrews 8:3-5*

Not only was the Messiah's sacrifice superior to the earthly sacrifices done in the temple in Jerusalem, but His covenant is superior to the covenant of Moses as well. His new covenant replaces the old covenant because there were problems with that old covenant. Namely, that it could condemn you for sinning, but it could not provide any means of reconciliation toward God for mankind.

"But now hath He obtained a more excellent ministry, by how much also He is the mediator of a better covenant, which was established upon better promises. For if that first covenant had been faultless, then should no place have been sought for the second." *Hebrews 8:6-7*

That new covenant needs to replace the old to bring a way of reconciliation. This Melchizedekian covenant was prophesied by the prophet Jeremiah.

"Behold, the days come, saith the LORD, that I will make a new covenant with the house of Israel, and with the house of Judah: Not according to the covenant that I made with their fathers in the day that I took them by the hand to bring them out of the land of Egypt; which My covenant they brake, although I was an husband unto them, saith the LORD: But this shall be the covenant that I will make with the house of Israel; After those days, saith the LORD, I will put

Ancient Order of Melchizedek

> My law in their inward parts, and write it in their hearts; and will be their God, and they shall be My people. And they shall teach no more every man his neighbour, and every man his brother, saying, Know the LORD: for they shall all know Me, from the least of them unto the greatest of them, saith the LORD: for I will forgive their iniquity, and I will remember their sin no more." *Jeremiah 31:31-34*

Paul quotes this passage from Jeremiah explaining it this way. There is a fault in them and the Law. God will bring a new covenant that is completely different from the one that was given on Mount Sinai.

> "For finding fault with them, He saith, Behold, the days come, saith the Lord, when I will make a new covenant with the house of Israel and with the house of Judah: Not according to the covenant that I made with their fathers in the day when I took them by the hand to lead them out of the land of Egypt; because they continued not in My covenant, and I regarded them not, saith the Lord." *Hebrews 8:8-9*

This covenant will be placed in their hearts. The apostle Paul calls this the "new man," in Ephesians 4. The new man is a new nature that all Christians have. That does not mean we cannot fall into sin, but that our new nature wants to follow God's ways instead of sinning. Our old man is still present and wants to sin.

Hebrews 8

"For this is the covenant that I will make with the house of Israel after those days, saith the Lord; I will put my laws into their mind, and write them in their hearts: and I will be to them a God, and they shall be to Me a people:" *Hebrews 8:10*

There is a Dead Sea Scroll called the *Damascus Document*. In this scroll, the Essenes of Qumran call the new covenant the Covenant of Damascus. Many have wondered why. It has nothing to do with Damascus, Syria. Damascus is the Essene name for their city that we today call Qumran. The word "Damascus" is made up of two Hebrew words; "dam," meaning blood, and "mashaq" meaning "heir" or "stronghold." The new covenant of Damascus is the new covenant of the blood heir. It is the new covenant of the Messiah!

This new covenant was given at Pentecost with the Holy Spirit for all who would accept it. Many rejected it and became apostate. In the millennial kingdom the nation of Israel will corporately accept Jesus as the promised Messiah and enter into the new covenant. This is why we have Christians today who are in the new covenant and orthodox Jews who are not yet in the new covenant.

"And they shall not teach every man his neighbour, and every man his brother, saying, Know the Lord: for all shall know Me, from the least to the greatest. For I will be merciful to their unrighteousness, and their sins and their iniquities will I remember no more." *Hebrews 8:11-12*

Ancient Order of Melchizedek

Paul ends the chapter by stating that the fact that there is a new covenant means that there was an old covenant. The old covenant was for the Age of Torah according to the scrolls, and the new covenant is for the Age of Grace. If the Age of Torah ended in AD 75 as predicted by the school of Elijah, and the epistle to the Hebrews was written in the 50's AD, then the old covenant vanished away within fifteen years of the writing of this epistle. This is exactly what the apostle Paul says.

> "In that He saith, A new covenant, He hath made the first old. Now that which decayeth and waxeth old is ready to vanish away." *Hebrews 8:13*

Conclusion

In this chapter we learned that Jesus is our eternal high priest. He is of the Order of Melchizedek and not of the Order of Levi (also called the Order of Aaron). The old Order of Levi was done away with in AD 75 at the end of the Age of Torah. The old priesthood with its old covenant could point out sin and condemn the guilty but could do nothing to fix the problem. The new covenant fixed the problem and reconciled us to God. Now all believers, both Jew and Gentile, have the Holy Spirit dwelling in them which gives them a new nature. Our new nature wants to serve God, but our old nature is still present in us and can lead us back into sin.

King – Priests

Christians are people who follow Jesus Christ and His teachings. Jesus, the Messiah, is our great high priest and He is our King. The apostle Paul teaches us that Jesus is our eternal Melchizedekian priest. Christians are not one ethnic group, but are groups of people from every walk of life. We have come together to form a new nation, a people united by Jesus Christ Himself. Originally this was supposed to start with the nation of Israel.

> "Now therefore, if ye will obey My voice indeed, and keep My covenant, then ye shall be a peculiar treasure unto Me above all people: for all the earth is Mine: And ye shall be unto Me a kingdom of priests, and an holy nation. These are the words which thou shalt speak unto the children of Israel."
> *Exodus 19:5-6*

The Gentiles would have been added to them, but they apostatized. God used the prophet Hosea to show that He would no longer have mercy toward His people, but would show mercy to another people. To signify this, Hosea was to name his daughter Lo-Ruhamah meaning "no mercy."

> "And she conceived again, and bare a daughter. And God said unto him, Call her name Lo-ruhamah: for I will no more have mercy upon the house of Israel; but I will utterly take them away. But I will have

mercy upon the house of Judah, and will save them by the LORD their God, and will not save them by bow, nor by sword, nor by battle, by horses, nor by horsemen." *Hosea 1:6-7*

God also instructed Hosea to name his next child "Lo-Ammi" which means "not my people." God was making Hosea's son a prophecy that the nation of Israel would rebel against God and that God would no longer call them His people. But much later in time, God gathered together groups of peoples from all nations and they formed a new "people of God."

"...she conceived, and bare a son. Then said God, Call his name Lo-ammi: for ye are not My people, and I will not be your God. Yet the number of the children of Israel shall be as the sand of the sea, which cannot be measured nor numbered; and it shall come to pass, that in the place where it was said unto them, Ye are not My people, there it shall be said unto them, Ye are the sons of the living God." *Hosea 1:8b-10*

The apostle John referenced this "people of God" when writing to the seven churches of Asia. John says we (the Christians) are that prophesied kingdom of priests.

"John, to the seven churches which are in Asia: Grace be unto you, and peace, from Him which is, and which was, and which is to come; and from the seven Spirits which are before His throne; And from

King-Priests

Jesus Christ, who is the faithful witness, and the first begotten of the dead, and the prince of the kings of the earth. Unto Him that loved us, and washed us from our sins in His own blood, And hath made us kings and priests unto God and His Father; to Him be glory and dominion for ever and ever. Amen." *Revelation 1:4-6*

The apostle Peter agreed with the apostle John by saying that the Gentile believers that were without Christ in the world have now become a "royal priesthood" and a "holy nation."

"But ye are a chosen generation, a royal priesthood, an holy nation, a peculiar people; that ye should shew forth the praises of Him who hath called you out of darkness into His marvellous light: Which in time past were not a people, but are now the people of God: which had not obtained mercy, but now have obtained mercy. Dearly beloved, I beseech you as strangers and pilgrims, abstain from fleshly lusts, which war against the soul;" *1 Peter 2:9-11*

We know that Jesus is our eternal high priest. He will never pass the priesthood over to another. So, in what sense are we priests and kings with Him? Christians do not offer animal sacrifices as a priest might do, we do not give orders to be obeyed as a king would do, and very few of us give new prophecies by the leading of the Holy Spirit. So, in what sense are we kings, priests, and prophets?

Ancient Order of Melchizedek

As Kings

We represent the King by being His ambassadors. This means we do not judge or give orders, but we teach *His* judgments and teach *His* orders. Paul tells Timothy to

> "preach the Word, be instant in season and out of season, reprove, rebuke, exhort with all long-suffering and doctrine. For a time will be when they will not endure sound doctrine, but they will heap up teachers to themselves according to their own lusts, tickling the ear. And they will turn away their ears from the truth and will be turned to myths. But you watch in all things, endure afflictions, do the work of an evangelist, fully carry out your ministry."
> *2 Timothy 4:2-5 MKJV*

"For the grace of God that bringeth salvation hath appeared to all men, Teaching us that, denying ungodliness and worldly lusts, we should live soberly, righteously, and godly, in this present world; Looking for that blessed hope, and the glorious appearing of the great God and our Saviour Jesus Christ; Who gave Himself for us, that He might redeem us from all iniquity, and purify unto Himself a peculiar people, zealous of good works. These things speak, and exhort, and rebuke with all authority. Let no man despise thee." *Titus 2:11-15*

As Priests

A priest acts as an intercessor to help people come before the Lord. As priests we pray with unbelievers to lead them

King-Priests

to the Lord. We pray with believers for peace, safety, and the guidance of the Holy Spirit in their lives. We listen and try to help where God allows us to.

"Pray without ceasing. In everything give thanks, for this is the will of God in Christ Jesus toward you." *1 Thessalonians 5:17-18 LITV*

"First of all then, I exhort that petitions, prayers, supplications, and thanksgivings be made on behalf of all men, for kings and all the ones being in high position, that we may lead a tranquil and quiet existence in all godliness and dignity. For this is good and acceptable before God our Savior, who desires all men to be saved and to come to a full knowledge of truth." *1 Timothy 2:1-4 LITV*

"Let love be without dissimulation. Abhor that which is evil; cleave to that which is good. Be kindly affectioned one to another with brotherly love; in honour preferring one another; Not slothful in business; fervent in spirit; serving the Lord; Rejoicing in hope; patient in tribulation; continuing instant in prayer; Distributing to the necessity of saints; given to hospitality. Bless them which persecute you: bless, and curse not. Rejoice with them that do rejoice, and weep with them that weep. Be of the same mind one toward another." *Romans 12:9-16a*

Ancient Order of Melchizedek

> "By Him, then, let us offer the sacrifice of praise to God continually, that is, the fruit of our lips, confessing His name. But do not forget to do good and to share, for with such sacrifices God is well pleased." *Hebrews 13:15-16 MKJV*

As Prophets
The prophet is the opposite of the king. He doesn't tell you what you must do for God, but he tells you what God is doing for mankind. He instructs in history and future history, which is called prophecy. To be a "son of the prophets" means to carefully study all the prophecies.

> "Study earnestly to present yourself approved to God, a workman that does not need to be ashamed, rightly dividing the Word of Truth."
> *2 Timothy 2:15 MKJV*

> "Do not despise prophecies. Test all things, hold fast the good." *1 Thessalonians 5:20-21 LITV*

As I said before, the Essenes believed they were led directly by the Holy Spirit. The community in Qumran called themselves "Yahad." This is a contraction of two Hebrew words. "Yah" is the name of God and "ehad" means "one" in the sense of one group of brothers. So, the name "Yahad" means a group of believers united together as one by the leading of the Holy Spirit.

King-Priests

Some even teach that *Yahovah* is a name for the Father, *Yeshua* is a name for the Son, and *Yah* is a name for the Holy Spirit.

Zadok Priests in the Millennium

If the order of Levi has been abolished, then why does the prophet Ezekiel say that there will be Zadok priests (of the order of Levi) serving in a rebuilt temple in Jerusalem during the one-thousand-year reign of Jesus Christ?

"It shall be for the priests that are sanctified of the sons of Zadok; which have kept My charge, which went not astray when the children of Israel went astray, as the Levites went astray." *Ezekiel 48:11*

I think the answer to this is found in the Dead Sea Scrolls known as the *Damascus Document* and the *Community Rule*.

They describe that the Pentecost dates remain the same, but the rituals and dispensations change. On a Pentecost, believers received the Noahide Covenant (Genesis 9), the Law of Moses on Mount Sinai (Exodus 19), and the giving of the New Covenant of Grace (Acts 2).

In addition to this, the scrolls teach the date of Passover remains the same, but the rituals and dispensations change. The texts describe that there was a ritual of bread and wine performed by Melchizedekian priests during the Age of Chaos (1-2000 AM). When the covenant of Moses came, the Melchizedekian ritual was replaced with what we know as the Passover Seder ritual. They predicted that during the next age, the Age of Grace, the ritual would change again. Bread and wine would still be used, but the Messiah Himself, would change the ritual. This happened. Today this modified ritual is called Christian communion. They went on to say that after the Second Coming, the Messiah would again change the ritual to point to the New Covenant of the Kingdom Age. One reason given is that there would be not only Jews and Gentiles observing the ritual, but also the Messiah Himself, along with His angels and His immortal ones. The immortal ones would be the Church Age Christians who were resurrected or raptured and at that time rule with the Messiah in His kingdom. Amazing, isn't it?

So, back to the original question: Why Zadok priests? There is something in that new ritual that points to the Messiah and His kingdom. All we really know is that at that point in time the rituals will not be the same as they were back in the days of Moses. We shall see.

Conclusion
Pulling together the teachings from the apostles and the Dead Sea Scrolls, we can see that the Messiah is the one and only Melchizedekian high priest and He will be that for all of eternity. We are His representatives on earth. We are king-priest-prophets only in the sense of representing Him. We represent Him as kings by teaching His commands. We represent Him as priests by counseling nonbelievers to accept Him as their Savior and to counsel believers in the whole council of God. We represent Him as prophets when

we teach the prophecies. Sometimes the Holy Spirit may give us a word of wisdom or knowledge for our brothers.

God equips Christians with spiritual gifts that help them do the things He commands. None of us have all gifts and none of us can do everything effectively. Some have ministries of teaching. Others have ministries of consolation, counseling, and evangelism. Still others have prophetical gifts. If you are not a believer, you should become one. If you are a believer, you need to find out what your spiritual gift is and begin exercising it.

Ancient Order of Melchizedek

Melchizedekian Prophecy

The Patriarchs

The Essenes taught that the ancient patriarchs, Adam through Aaron, wrote testaments for their children. These testaments contain moral wisdom and Messianic prophecy. The Pharisees agreed that these patriarchal texts did exist, but said they were lost long ago. Nothing is ever lost except that which you choose to throw away because it does not fit your doctrine. The Essenes rejected the Pharisee's Oral Torah because of what is taught in the Testaments of the Patriarchs. The Pharisees reject the Essene testaments because of what their Oral Torah says. Jesus said the Pharisees' "Traditions of the Elders," their Oral Torah, makes void the Word of God.

First Chronicles states there were those of the tribe of Issachar who understood the division of the four "ages," which means they were serious students of the biblical and patriarchal prophecies. They were called the "sons of the prophets."

> "And of the children of Issachar, which were men that had understanding of the times, to know what Israel ought to do; the heads of them were two hundred; and all their brethren were at their commandment." *1 Chronicles 12:32*

This is also referred to as the "tabernacle of David." This tabernacle, or school, of David followed the Law and

The Patriarchs

prophets correctly. With the rise of the Sadducees and Pharisees, an apostate form of Judaism was established. But with the advent of the Messiah, all was restored.

"After this I will return, and will build again the tabernacle of David, which is fallen down; and I will build again the ruins thereof, and I will set it up: That the residue of men might seek after the Lord, and all the Gentiles, upon whom My name is called, saith the Lord, who doeth all these things. Known unto God are all His works from the beginning of the world [Age]." *Acts 15:16-18*

The following is a list of the major prophecies given by the biblical patriarchs. For a complete study in the fragments of the Testaments of the Patriarchs found in the Dead Sea Scrolls, see the book *Ancient Testaments of the Patriarchs* by this author.

Messiah is the Son of God, *Levi 4*
Messiah is God incarnate, *Simeon 6, 7; Zebulun 9; Naphtali 8; Asher 7*; *Benjamin 10*
Levi's priesthood is only until Messiah, *Reuben 6; Levi 4, 5; Benjamin 9*
Levi's ordinances and sacrifices are only until Messiah *Reuben 6*
Tribes rebel against Judah and Levi, *Reuben 6* and *Dan 5*
Messiah is the seed of Judah, *Reuben 6; Judah 24; Gad 8*
Messiah is virgin-born, *Joseph 19*
We worship the Messiah, *Reuben 6*
Messiah is an everlasting King, *Reuben 6; Joseph 19*

Ancient Order of Melchizedek

Messiah dies for us, *Reuben 6*
Physical resurrection, *Simeon 6; Judah 25; Zebulun 10; Benjamin 10*
Messiah brings salvation, *Simeon 6; Levi 4; Asher 7; Joseph 19; Benjamin 3*
Levites crucify the Messiah, *Levi 4, 16; Aaron 4, 6; Benjamin 9*
There will be two expulsions, *Levi 15; Zebulun 9; Naphtali 4; Asher 7*
Messiah resurrects, *Levi 16*
Messiah ascends, *Levi 18*
Messiah creates a new priesthood, *Levi 18; Aaron 4*
Book of Enoch mentioned, *Levi 16; Judah 18; Zebulun 3; Naphtali 4; Benjamin 9*
The Writings of the Fathers existed, *Zebulun 9; Kohath 2*
Messiah appears in Zebulun, *Zebulun 9*
New Jerusalem mentioned, *Dan 5*
Old Jerusalem mentioned, *Jacob 2*
The Watchers mentioned, *Naphtali 3*
Messiah's priesthood is eternal, *Amram-4Q547; Aaron 4*
Veil of the Temple Rent, *Benjamin 9*

For the purpose of our study, we want to show what the patriarchs teach about (1) the Messiah, (2) the apostasy at the time of the first coming of the Messiah, and (3) the new covenant that the Messiah would bring at the beginning of the Age of Grace.

The Messiah

In this section we will see the prophecies that the scrolls reveal about the Messiah Himself.

1. The Messiah will be God incarnate.
2. Believers will worship the Messiah as God.
3. He will be born of a virgin.
4. He will die for our sins to reconcile us to God.

Messiah is God Incarnate

"Then the world will rest from war and Shem will be glorified, because the Lord God, the Mighty One of Israel, will appear upon earth as man, and save the seed of Adam." *Testament of Simeon, 6*

"After these things the Lord Himself will arise to you. The light of righteousness, healing, and compassion will be in His wings. He will redeem all captivity of the sons of men from Belial, and every spirit of error will be trodden down. He will bring back all the nations to zeal for Him, and you will see God in the fashion of a man whom the Lord will choose." *Testament of Zebulun, 9*

"For through Judah will salvation arise to Israel, and Jacob will be blessed through him. For through his tribe God will be seen dwelling among men on the

earth, to save the race of Israel. He will gather together the righteous from the Gentiles."
Testament of Naphtali, 8

"...until the Most High will visit the earth. He will come as man, eating and drinking with men, and in peace He will break the head of the dragon through water. He will save Israel and all nations, God speaking in the person of man. Therefore, teach these things to your children, so they will not disobey Him;" *Testament of Naphtali, 8*

"The Lord will judge Israel first, even for the wrong they did unto Him; for when He appeared as a deliverer, God in the flesh, they did not believe Him. Then He will judge all the Gentiles, as many as did not believe Him when He appeared on earth. He will reprove Israel among the chosen ones of the Gentiles, even as He reproved Esau among the Midianites..." *Testament of Benjamin, 10*

Believers Will Worship the Messiah as God.

"For He will bless Israel; and specially Judah, because the Lord chose him to rule over all the people. We will worship his Seed, because He will die for us in wars visible and invisible, and will be among you an everlasting king."
Testament of Reuben, 6

The Messiah

Messiah will be Virgin Born
The book of Enoch hints at the virgin birth of the Messiah.

> "They will be downcast of countenance and pain will seize them when they see that Son of Man sitting on the throne of His glory."
> *Ancient Book of Enoch 62:5*

Some manuscripts of Enoch replace "Son of Man," the common messianic title, with the more uncommon messianic title of "Son of Woman." The son of woman carries the same meaning as the "seed of the woman" as seen in Genesis.

> "And I will put enmity between thee and the woman, and between thy seed and her seed; it shall bruise thy head, and thou shalt bruise His heel."
> *Genesis 3:15*

The idioms "son of woman" and "seed of woman" both mean virgin born. The prophet Isaiah makes this clearer.

> "Therefore the Lord Himself shall give you a sign; Behold, a virgin shall conceive, and bear a son, and shall call His name Immanuel."
> *Isaiah 7:14*

Another clear reference is in the Testament of Joseph 19.

> "Hear also, my children, the visions which I saw. There were twelve deer feeding, and the nine were

divided and scattered in the land, likewise also the three. I saw that from Judah was born a virgin wearing a linen garment, and from her went forth a Lamb, without spot, and on His left hand there was a lion. All the beasts rushed against Him, and the Lamb overcame them, destroyed them, and trampled them under foot. Because of Him, the angels, men, and all the earth rejoiced. These things will take place in their season, in the last days. Therefore, my children, observe the commandments of the Lord, and honor Judah and Levi. From them will rise unto you the Lamb of God, by grace saving all the Gentiles and Israel. For His kingdom is an everlasting kingdom, which will not be shaken; but my kingdom among you will come to an end as a watcher's hammock, which after the summer will not appear."

Testament of Joseph 19

According to Hippolytus' record of the School of the Prophets, Nathan was a leader of the school and therefore his writings would have been in the Dead Sea Scrolls. No copy has yet been found in the Judean hills, but I am sure there will be in the future. In the meantime, we will look at fragments of the Book of Nathan that clearly prove the virgin birth of the Messiah. This first fragment records part of a vision that King David saw about the Messiah and His mother. Notice that here, David calls the incarnation the "mystery of Yahweh," while the apostle Paul in 1 Timothy 3:16 calls this the "mystery of godliness."

The Messiah

"I admonish you, O my son, Solomon. Carry out my will and remember the *Mystery of Yahweh* that I saw in a vision (wonders) from the Lord about His virgin mother, who is to emerge from our tribe."
Fragment of the Testament of Nathan

This second portion is Nathan's own vision about the virgin birth. Notice Nathan does not use any word for virgin so it cannot be debated whether the word could mean virgin or just young woman. The description is clear. A young woman who has never been with a man *is* a virgin! Her child is the Lord of the earth. Adam and Noah were the only kings of the whole earth and they both lost control of it. This future king of the world will not lose control of it.

"I saw one, a maiden and without touch of man, and a man child in her arms, and that was the Lord of the earth unto the ends of the earth."
Fragment of the Testament of Nathan

Messiah will Die for our Sins to Reconcile us to God
The Messiah dies for us and this makes salvation possible to all mankind

"We will worship his Seed, because He will die for us in wars visible and invisible, and will be among you an everlasting king." *Testament of Reuben 6*

"Therefore, my children, observe the commandments of the Lord, and honor Judah and Levi. From them will rise unto you the Lamb of God,

by grace saving all the Gentiles and Israel. For His kingdom is an everlasting kingdom..."
Testament of Joseph 19

"In you will be fulfilled the prophecy of heaven concerning the Lamb of God, even the Savior of the world. He will be delivered up spotless for transgressors. He will be sinless, yet put to death for ungodly men in the blood of the covenant, for the salvation of the Gentiles and of Israel. He will destroy Belial, and them that serve him."
Testament of Benjamin 3

"The LORD will cast their lot amid the portions of Melchizedek, who will make them repent and will proclaim freedom to them, to free them from the debt of all their iniquities." *11QMelchizedek*

The Apostasy

The apostasy that the scrolls describe can be broken down into several points.

1. The Levites will reject the Messiah.
2. Messiah will be crucified.
3. God will end the Levitical priesthood.
4. The apostasy will bring total madness.
5. The veil in the temple will be torn in two.

The Levites Reject the Messiah and Crucify Him

"You and all your seed will be blessed until the Lord visits all the heathen in the tender mercies of His Son, even forever. Nevertheless, your sons will lay hands upon Him to crucify Him. Therefore, you have been given counsel and understanding to instruct your sons about Him, because he who blesses Him will be blessed, but they that curse Him will perish." *Testament of Levi, 4*

"I have also learned in the book of Enoch that for seventy weeks you will go astray, will profane the priesthood, pollute the sacrifices, corrupt the law, and ignore the words of the prophets. In perverseness, you will persecute righteous men, hate the godly, and abhor the words of the faithful. The man who renews the law in the power of the Most

Ancient Order of Melchizedek

High you will call a deceiver. At last, as you suppose, you will slay Him, not understanding His resurrection, wickedly taking upon your own heads the innocent blood. Because of Him will your holy places be desolate, polluted even to the ground, and you will have no place that is clean; but you will be among the Gentiles a curse and a dispersion, until He will again look on you, and in pity will take you to Himself through faith and water."
Testament of Levi, 16

"Let not the nail touch him. Then you will raise up for your father a name of rejoicing and for all your brothers a firm foundation. You will understand and rejoice in the eternal light and you will not be one whom God hates." *Testament of Aaron, Col. 6*

God Ends the Levitical Priesthood

"Obey Levi, because he will know the law of the Lord, and will create ordinances for judgment and sacrifice for all Israel until the time of Messiah, the High Priest whom the Lord has declared."
Testament of Reuben, 6

"You and all your seed will be blessed until the Lord visits all the heathen in the tender mercies of His Son, even forever. Nevertheless, your sons will lay hands upon Him to crucify Him." *Testament of Levi 4*

The Apostasy

"He said to me, 'Levi, I have given you the blessings of the priesthood until I will come and sojourn in the midst of Israel.'" *Testament of Levi 5*

"The words of the righteous Enoch teach that even your descendants will practice evil. They will commit fornication like the fornication of Sodom, and all but a few will perish, and will multiply inordinate lusts with women; and the kingdom of the Lord will not be among you, for immediately He will take it away." *Testament of Benjamin 9*

The Apostasy Brings Total Madness

"In their days, pride will cause many to act wickedly against the covenant and become the slaves of foreign things. Israel will be rent asunder in that generation, each man fighting against his neighbor over the Torah and the Covenant. I will send hunger upon the land, but not for bread or water, but to hear the Word of the Lord." *4Q385a fragment 5*

"...at the completion of ten jubilees, Israel will be walking in madness..." *4Q387*

The Sign of the Veil of the Temple

The scrolls speak of a beautiful Jewish temple being the glory for both Jews and Gentiles. But one prediction says that when the Levites reject the Messiah, God would reject and end the Levitical priesthood. The public sign of this would be the veil in the temple would be torn in two.

Ancient Order of Melchizedek

> "Nevertheless, the temple of God will be built in your portion, and will be glorious among you. For He will take it, and the twelve tribes will be gathered together there, and all the Gentiles, until the Most High will send forth His salvation in the visitation of His only-begotten One. He will enter into the front of the temple, and there will the Lord be treated with outrage, and He will be lifted up on a tree. The veil of the temple will be rent, and the Spirit of God will descend upon the Gentiles as fire poured forth."
> *Testament of Benjamin 9*

The New Testament does not tell us this was predicted, but it does speak of its fulfillment.

> "Jesus, when he had cried again with a loud voice, yielded up the ghost. And, behold, the veil of the temple was rent in twain from the top to the bottom; and the earth did quake, and the rocks rent;"
> *Matthew 27:50-51*

Messiah's Covenant / Priesthood

The scrolls also reveal several points about the covenant and priesthood that the Messiah brings at His first coming.

1. Messiah's Covenant replaces Levi's.
2. Messiah's Covenant would be a Gentile one.
3. Messiah's Priesthood / Covenant is eternal.
4. There would be a New Testament.

Messiah's Covenant / Priesthood Replaces Levi's
When Levi was given the priesthood, he understood that his priesthood was different from the previous Melchizedekian priesthood and when the Messiah came the priesthood would change again. It would become a Gentile priesthood headed by the Messiah who would be from the tribe of Judah, not the tribe of Levi. Levi was told in a dream the following:

> "They said to me, 'Levi, your seed [the priesthood] will be divided into three branches, for a sign of the glory of the Lord who is to come. The first will be he who has been faithful; no portion will be greater than his. The second will be in the priesthood. The third—a new name will be called over Him, because He will arise as King from Judah, and will establish a new priesthood, after the fashion of the Gentiles, to all the Gentiles. His appearing will be unutterable, as of an

Ancient Order of Melchizedek

> exalted prophet of the seed of Abraham our father."
> *Testament of Levi 8*

The Mosaic Covenant Replaced
Levi's priesthood would only exist until Messiah came.

> "For the Lord made Levi, Judah, Dan, Joseph, and me rulers over you. Therefore, I command you to obey Levi, because he will know the law of the Lord, and will create ordinances for judgment and sacrifice for all Israel until the time of Messiah, the High Priest whom the Lord has declared."
> *Testament of Reuben, 6*

Age of Grace
The School of Elijah taught a dispensational view of history, according to an ancient commentary on Elijah's school called the *Tanna Eliyahu*. They divided history into four "Ages." First was the "Age of Chaos." Its name was taken from Genesis 1:2 (the earth was "without form" or in chaos). This was the age spanning from Creation to when God called Abraham. The second was called the "Age of Torah." This was the age of temples and sacrifices. It was supposed to last until the first coming of the Messiah. The Messiah would usher in the third age called the "Age of Grace." The Dead Sea Scrolls talk about the Messiah's New Covenant coming in the Age of Grace. One such document is called the *Community Rule*. It looks forward to the next age when Jews and Gentiles can enter the New Covenant together. The *Community Rule* actually says they

Messiah's Covenant / Priesthood

will welcome the Gentiles into the Kingdom when the Age of Grace starts.

> "welcome all those who freely choose to obey God's decrees and enter the Covenant of Grace."
> *Community Rule, section 1*

The Essenes believed the Messiah's first coming would start this new Age of Grace.

The Messiah's New Eternal Priesthood

When the Messiah comes, the New Covenant He would create will last forever.

> "and will be chosen as a priest forever..."
> *Testament of Amram, 4Q547*

> "...His wisdom will be great. He will make atonement for all the children of His generation. He will be sent to all the sons of His [generation]. His word will be as the word of heaven, and His teaching will be in accordance with the will of God. His eternal sun will burn bright. The fire will be kindled in all the corners of the earth. It will shine into the darkness. Then the darkness will vanish from the earth and the deep darkness from the dry land. They will speak many words against Him. There will be numerous lies. They will invent stories about Him. They will say shameful things about Him. He will overthrow His evil generation and there will be great wrath. When He arises, there will be falsehood and

violence, and the people will wander astray in His days and be confounded."
Testament of Amram, Col. 4

Messiah is an Everlasting King

"Therefore, my children, observe the commandments of the Lord, and honor Judah and Levi. From them will rise unto you the Lamb of God, by grace saving all the Gentiles and Israel. For His kingdom is an everlasting kingdom, which will not be shaken; but my kingdom among you will come to an end as a watcher's hammock, which after the summer will not appear." *Testament of Joseph 19*

Messiah Creates a New Priesthood

"... His wisdom will be great. He will make atonement for all the children of His generation. He will be sent to all the sons of His [generation]. His word will be as the word of heaven, and His teaching will be in accordance with the will of God. His eternal sun will burn bright. The fire will be kindled in all the corners of the earth. It will shine into the darkness. Then the darkness will vanish from the earth and the deep darkness from the dry land. They will speak many words against Him. There will be numerous lies. They will invent stories about Him. They will say shameful things about Him. He will overthrow His evil generation and there will be great wrath. When He arises, there will be falsehood and

violence, and the people will wander astray in His days and be confounded."
Testament of Aaron, Col. 4

"...After the Lord punishes them, He will raise up to the priesthood a new Priest, to whom all the words of the Lord will be revealed... He will give the majesty of the Lord to His sons in truth for evermore; and there will none succeed Him for all generations, even forever. In His priesthood the Gentiles will be multiplied in knowledge on the earth and enlightened through the grace of the Lord. In His priesthood all sin will come to an end, the lawless will rest from evil, and the just will rest in Him."
Testament of Levi 18

The New Testament Scriptures

It is very fascinating that not only do we have the prediction of a New Covenant and new priesthood, but there would also be a New Testament. Think about that for a moment. They hallowed the writings of the patriarchs as a revelation from God; a kind of pre-Old-Testament covenant. Then there would be a covenant written for the second age, the Age of Torah. This was written by Moses. At the beginning of the Age of Grace there would be another set of books that believers would live their lives by. We call this the New Testament.

"I will no longer be called a ravening wolf on account of your ravages, but a worker of the Lord, distributing food to them that work what is good. One will rise up from my seed in the latter times, beloved of the Lord, hearing His voice on the earth, enlightening with new knowledge all the Gentiles, bursting in on Israel for salvation with the light of knowledge, and tearing it away from them like a wolf, and giving it to the synagogue of the Gentiles. Until the consummation of the ages he will be in the synagogues of the Gentiles, and among their rulers, as a strain of music in the mouth of all; and he will be inscribed in the holy books, both his work and his word, and he will be a chosen one of God forever; and because of him my father Jacob instructed me, saying, 'He will fill up that which lacks from your tribe.'" *Testament of Benjamin 11*

The apostle Paul became aware of the prophecy that he (the predicted Benjamite) would become the apostle to the Gentiles. His life (the Book of Acts) and his teachings (the epistles of Paul) would be written down and placed in a New Testament which would be located in the synagogue of the Gentiles (the Christian church) for all time.

Let me make this clear. According to the Dead Sea Scrolls, if we are not sure about doctrine, all the answers will be written in the epistles of Paul!

"...until the Messiah of righteousness comes, the branch of David, for to Him and His children have been given the covenant of the kingship of His people for everlasting generations..." *4Q252 Col. 5*

The Date of the First Coming

There is another Dead Sea Scroll referenced as 11QMelchizedek. It starts out explaining that the Old Testament law of the Jubilee period of debt forgiveness is actually a concealed prophecy about the coming of the Messiah. He would forgive the debts of our sin. This would reconcile us to God the Father. The Messiah is called Melchizedek because He is the tenth and final Melchizedekian priest and He begins the new order of the Age of Grace.

"Moses said, 'In the year of the jubilee, each of you will be freed to return home [Lev. 25:13]' and he described how, saying, 'Now this is the manner of the release: Let every creditor remit what he has lent his neighbor. He shall not press his neighbor or his brother for repayment, for the LORD's release has been proclaimed [Deut. 15:2].' Its interpretation pertains to the end of days. The captives Moses speaks of are those whom Isaiah says, 'To proclaim freedom to the captives [Isa. 61:1].' Its interpretation is that the LORD will assign those freed to the sons of heaven and the lot of Melchizedek. Even those, whose teachers had deliberately hidden and kept secret from them the truth about their inheritance through Melchizedek. The LORD will cast their lot amid the portions of Melchizedek, who will make them return [or repent] and will proclaim freedom to them, to free them from the debt of all their iniquities." *11QMelchizedek*

Now notice what it says about the timing of the arrival of the Messiah, Melchizedek, will die for our sins.

"This event will take place in the first week of the jubilee that occurs after the ninth jubilee." *11QMelchizedek*

Let's break this down. There are several ways to figure the timeline and we have written about this in many books, the *Ancient Seder Olam*, the *Ancient Dead Sea Scroll Calendar*, *Ancient Post-flood History*, etc. Basically, Abraham was called when he was fifty-two years old. That was the turn of the age, the year 2000 AM (two thousand years exactly from Creation to Abraham's call). The second two thousand years lasted from Abraham's call to just past the destruction of the Jewish temples. The Jerusalem temple was destroyed in AD 70 and the Alexandrian temple was shut down in AD 73. The end of the age was AD 75 on their calendar. An age lasts two thousand years. An age is made up of four five-hundred-year periods called "onahs." Each five-hundred-year period is made up of ten fifty-year periods called "jubilees." Each jubilee is made up of seven seven-year periods called "shemitahs." There are seven shemitahs and then a jubilee year, making fifty total.

So, if the end of the age is AD 75, that would be the end of the tenth jubilee. One jubilee back would be the end of the

Date of the First Coming

ninth jubilee or AD 25. The text says one shemitah after the end of the ninth jubilee, so, AD 25 plus seven years would bring us to AD 32. This is the year the Melchizedekian Messiah, Jesus Christ, died for our sins.

Next, we see the Messiah creates a "Day of Grace" also known as the "Age of Grace."

> "Now the Day of Atonement is the end of the tenth jubilee, when atonement (is made) for all the sons of heaven, for the men of the lot of Melchizedek... It is the time of Melchizedek's 'Day of Grace.' He will, by His strength, raise up the holy ones of God to execute judgment as it has been written concerning Him in the songs of David, as it says, 'Elohim stands in the divine assembly, in the midst of Elohim He judges [Ps 82:1].' He said, 'Above it, to the heights, return. El will judge the nations [Ps 7:8-9].' When he said, 'How long will you judge unjustly and show impartiality to the wicked? Selah [Ps 82:2].' Its interpretation concerns Belial and the spirits of his lot who turn away from the commandments of El in wickedness. Melchizedek will exact the vengeances of the judgments of El..." *11QMelchizedek*

By the end of the age (the end of the tenth jubilee) vengeance will come to the nation of Israel. Both temples will be destroyed, and the time of animal sacrifices will come to an end.

Ancient Order of Melchizedek

This is interesting to me as a Christian trying to figure out the exact dates of prophecy. You could say the new age started with the birth of the Messiah at 2 BC, His death and the birth of the church in AD 32, the destruction of one of the temples in AD 70-73, the end of the age proper in AD 75, or the expulsion of the nation of Israel in AD 135. This needs further study. The Essenes went on to say that this Age of Grace is a fulfillment of several Old Testament prophecies. These same passages were quoted in the New Testament by Paul and Jesus Christ.

> "This is the 'Day of Peace' about which God spoke through Isaiah the prophet [52:7] who said, 'How beautiful on the mountains are the feet of the Messenger who proclaims peace, the Messenger of good who proclaims salvation, saying to Zion, "Your God reigns!"' Its interpretation is that the mountains are prophets' predictions about the Messenger and the Messenger is the one anointed of the Spirit about whom Daniel said, 'Until Messiah, the Prince, (there will be) seven weeks [Dan. 9:25].' He is the Messenger of good who proclaims salvation. He is the one about whom it is written, when it says, 'to comfort those who mourn... [Isa. 61:2-3],' to 'instruct them in all the ages of the world in truth.'"
> *11QMelchizedek*

His salvation is true for "all the ages of the world." It is for all time. Salvation has always been by faith in the Messiah and not works. A very important point is that they accepted

Date of the First Coming

the Messiah not only as their Melchizedekian priest but as God incarnate. The text says, "your God is Melchizedek."

"Zion is those who uphold the covenant, those who turn aside from walking in the ways of the people. But 'your God' is Melchizedek, who will save them from the hand of Belial." *11QMelchizedek*

The very last part begins to speak of the time of the end of our age when the trumpet is blown, and the Rapture / Resurrection occurs. Unfortunately, it is too fragmented to give us a date or record the sequence of the events.

"As for that which he has said, 'You will blow the signal-horn in the seventh month [Lev 23:24; 25:9].' …the divisions of the times…"
11QMelchizedek

Conclusion

In Daniel 9 the Scriptures clearly reveal the Messiah's death in AD 32. Separate from that we have the Dead Sea Scroll 11QMelchizedek that gives us the exact year of the Messiah's death. It also reveals that His death is a work of the Father to pay for our sin nature and reconcile us to God. It is truly amazing that the Zadok priests would have the exact same theology as the Christian church.

Ancient Order of Melchizedek

Other Books by Ken Johnson, Th.D.

- **Ancient Post-Flood History**
  Historical documents that point to a biblical Creation.

- **Ancient Seder Olam**
  A Christian translation of the 2000-year-old scroll.

- **Ancient Prophecies Revealed**
  500 Prophecies listed in order of when they were fulfilled.

- **Ancient Book of Jasher**
  Referenced in Joshua 10:13; 2 Samuel 1:18; 2 Timothy 3:8.

- **Third Corinthians**
  Ancient Gnostics and the end of the world

- **Ancient Paganism**
  The sorcery of the fallen angels

- **The Rapture**
  The pretribulational Rapture of the church viewed from the Bible and the ancient church

- **Ancient Epistle of Barnabas**
  His life and teaching

- **The Ancient Church Fathers**
  What the disciples of the apostles taught

- **Ancient Book of Daniel**

- **Ancient Epistles of John and Jude**
- **Ancient Messianic Festivals**
  And the prophecies they reveal
- **Ancient Word of God**
- **Cults and the Trinity**
- **Ancient Book of Enoch**
- **Ancient Epistles of Timothy and Titus**
- **Fallen Angels**
- **Ancient Book of Jubilees**
- **The Gnostic Origins of Calvinism**
- **The Gnostic Origins of Roman Catholicism**
- **Demonic Gospels**
- **The Pre-Flood Origins of Astrology**
- **The End-Times by the Church Fathers**
- **Ancient Book of Gad the Seer**
- **Ancient Apocalypse of Ezra**
  Called 2 Esdras in the KJV
- **Ancient Testaments of the Patriarchs**
  Autobiographies from the Dead Sea Scrolls
- **Ancient Law of Kings**
  Noahide law
- **Ancient Origins of the Hebrew Roots Movement**
  The Noahide and Mosaic Laws as seen in the Dead Sea Scrolls

- **Ancient Origins of Modern Holidays**
- **Ancient Dead Sea Scroll Calendar**

- DVD 1 – **The Prophetic Timeline**
- DVD 2 – **The Church Age**

For more information,
visit us at: Biblefacts.org

Bibliography

Whiston, William, *The Works of Flavius Josephus*, London, Miller & Sowerby, 1987. Includes Antiquities of the Jews.

Ken Johnson, *Ancient Book of Jasher*, CreateSpace, 2008

Ken Johnson, *Ancient Book of Enoch*, CreateSpace, 2012

Eerdmans Publishing, *Ante-Nicene Fathers*, Eerdmans Publishing, 1886

Ken Johnson, *Ancient Dead Sea Scroll Calendar*, independent publisher, 2019

Ken Johnson, *Ancient Testaments of the Patriarchs*, independent publisher, 2017